New West African Literature

Edited by

KOLAWOLE OGUNGBESAN

Professor of English
Ahmadu Bello University, Zaria, Nigeria

LONDON
HEINEMANN
IBADAN   NAIROBI

Heinemann Educational Books Ltd
22 Bedford Square, London WC1B 3HH
PO Box 45314, Nairobi

EDINBURGH   MELBOURNE   AUCKLAND
HONG KONG   SINGAPORE   KUALA LUMPUR   NEW DELHI
KINGSTON   PORT OF SPAIN

Heinemann Educational Books (Nig.) Ltd.
Head Office: PMB 5205, Ighodaro Road, Ibadan
Phone:62060, 62061 Telex: 31113 Cable: HEBOOKS, Ibadan

Area Offices & Branches:
Ibadan Ikeja Akure Benin Ilorin Owerri Enugu Uyo
Port Harcourt Jos Maiduguri Makurdi Zaria Kano Minna

Hienemann Educational Books Inc.
4 Front Street, Exeter
New Hampshire 03833, USA

ISBN 0 435 91760 9 (cased)
ISBN 0 435 91761 7 (paper)

Set in Plantin V.I.P. 10pt
Printed in Great Britain
by Whitstable Litho Ltd
Whitstable, Kent

Contents

▼▼▼▼▼▼▼▼▼▼▼▼▼▼▼▼▼▼▼▼▼▼▼▼▼▼▼▼▼▼▼▼▼▼

Notes on Contributors

▼▼▼▼▼▼▼▼▼▼▼▼▼▼▼▼▼▼▼▼▼▼▼▼▼▼▼▼▼▼▼▼

KOFI ANYIDOHO, Ghanaian, studied at the University of Ghana, Legon and at Indiana University, Bloomington, USA. One of Ghana's younger writers, his poems have appeared in several journals and won various prizes. His volume of poems, *Elegy for Revolution*, has recently been published in the USA.

JAWA APRONTI, Ghanaian, studied at London University, Leeds University and the University of Ghana. His poetry has appeared in *Okyeame, Legon Observer, Transition*, and *Modern Poetry for Africa*. He has also published critical essays in several journals. He is Senior Research Fellow in Language and Literature at the Institute of African Studies, University of Ghana.

KWABENA BRITWUM, Ghanaian, studied at the University of Bordeaux, France, the University of Ghana, Legon, King's College, London, and the University of Caen, France, where he researched into the novels of Mongo Beti and Ferdinand Oyono. He has published a critical edition of Oyono's *Une vie de boy*, and has contributed articles on Beti, Oyono and Malraux to several journals. He is currently Senior Lecturer at the University of Ghana and is working on a book on Oyono.

FÍRINNE NÍ CHRÉACHÁIN-ADELUGBA, Irish, studied at Trinity College, Dublin, and the University of Texas where she did a comparative study of Kwei Armah and Ousmane Sembene. She is currently teaching French at Ahmadu Bello University, Zaria, Nigeria.

ROMANUS N. EGUDU, Nigerian, is currently Professor of English at the University of Benin, Nigeria. He was trained at the University of Nigeria, Nsukka, and Michigan State University, USA. He has edited books on Igbo poetry and various short stories. He has published *Four Modern West African Poets* (1977), *The Study of Poetry* (1977) and *Modern African Poetry and The African Predicament* (1978). He has also contributed articles and poems to numerous journals.

YUSUFU MAIANGWA, Nigerian, studied at Ahmadu Bello University, Zaria and the University of Toulouse-Le Mirail, France, where he took a PhD in contemporary French literature. A former President of the Modern Languages Association of Nigeria, he is currently Acting Head of Department of French at Ahmadu Bello University, Zaria, Nigeria.

AKANJI NASIRU, Nigerian, was educated at the University of Ibadan where he did a PhD in Theatre Arts on the subject, 'Communication and the Nigerian Drama in English'. After teaching Drama at Ahmadu Bello University, Zaria, he is now Head of the Cultural Section of the Council for Arts and Culture, Oyo State, Nigeria.

KOLAWOLE OGUNGBESAN, Nigerian, studied at the University of Ibadan and Indiana University, Bloomington, USA. He has published articles on African literature in numerous journals. He coedited, *A Celebration of Black and African Writing* with Bruce King and two poetry anthologies with David Woolger. His book, *The Writings of Peter Abrahams* has just been published in Britain. He was working on the novels of Nadine Gordimer. He was Professor and Head of the English Department at Ahmadu Bello University, Zaria, Nigeria when he died tragically early in 1979.

OLALERE OLADITAN, Nigerian, is currently lecturing at the University of Ife, Nigeria. He was educated at the University of Ibadan where he obtained a PhD on the subject, 'The Theme of Violence in the African Novel of French Expression'. He is at present working on a book on the Nigerian novel and another on the Nigerian military, 1966-1970.

NORMAN STOKLE, English, was educated at Syracuse University, New York, where he did a PhD on Camus. He has published books on Salacrou, Camus, modern French theatre, and has contributed essays on African literature to several books and journals. His book, *L'Afrique Noire Francophone*, an exploration of various aspects of the contemporary African scene, will be published shortly by Macmillan and Ahmadu Bello University Press. He is Chairman of Foreign Languages at the University of Tulsa, USA.

Introduction

▼▼▼▼▼▼▼▼▼▼▼▼▼▼▼▼▼▼▼▼▼▼▼▼▼▼▼▼▼▼▼▼▼▼▼▼

THE title of this collection of essays may prove troublesome. Why, or in what sense, *new*? For, by all accounts, African literature in the European languages is usually considered a post-Second World War phenomenon. Also, its primary concern, right from its inception, has been politics. Almost everyone among the first generation of African writers would recognize his own beginning in the following sentiments expressed by Chinua Achebe:

> At the university I read some appalling novels about Africa (including Joyce Cary's much praised *Mister Johnson*) and decided that the story we had to tell could not be told for us by anyone else no matter how well-intentioned. Although I did not set about it consciously in that solemn way, I now know that my first book, *Things Fall Apart*, was an act of atonement with my past, the ritual return and homage of a prodigal son.

At the initial stage virtually all the writers were content to affirm the worth of African civilizations. Indeed, cultural nationalism was a part of the anti-colonial campaign. But this mood remained tenable only as long as Africa continued to be a colony of Europe. Soon after political independence was won, African writing entered a new phase; its mood became totally different from, and in some instances was diametrically opposed to, the pre-independence mood of affirmation. Disillusion quickly set in when the writers discovered that the ruling élite was more interested in conserving its own dominance and in monopolizing the continent's natural resources than in improving the abject conditions of the common people. Gabriel Okara's *The Voice* (1964), Wole Soyinka's *The Interpreters* (1965) and Ayi Kwei Armah's *The Beautyful Ones Are Not Yet Born* (1968) were products of the writers' mood of disenchantment immediately after independence. But it soon became obvious that something more positive than righteous indignation or blank despair was needed to cope with the social malaise. Soyinka, always a useful barome-

ter for measuring the intellectual climate on the continent, proclaimed a
new era in an address to other African writers in 1967: 'It seems to me
that the time has now come when the African writer must have the
courage to determine what alone can be salvaged from the recurrent cycle
of human stupidity.'

This volume of essays treats, within the West African sub-region,
some of the literary works produced in this latest phase. One dominant
theme in all the essays is the writer's search for an appropriate response to
the political moment of his society. Because all the writers have been
involved in the dialectics of class struggle, each in his own way has
examined the methods by which his society can be saved from the
injustices of a capitalist-oriented society.

In 1971 the white South African writer Nadine Gordimer criticized
black African novelists for their obsession with analysing the corruption
in their societies instead of resolving the fate of these societies in terms of
profound social change:

> The ideology of African socialism, for example, may be a live issue at
> sessions of the OAU, but no creative writer in English has yet dealt
> with it. In African writers' interpretations, where African societies
> fail, the blame lies with the individual, the political ideology is hardly
> questioned. At most there is a concurrence of opinion that the Western
> brand of democracy may not do, and that tribalism must be abolished
> if it cannot be pressed into the service of unity in any other way. So far,
> the independent African state is visualized by its novelists as a capital-
> ist one in which, while the lot of the ordinary people will be improved
> gradually, no revolutionary change in their status – such as is being
> attempted by Julius Nyerere in Tanzania – is reflected. For this
> reason, the post-colonial political novel like the political novel of the
> colonial struggle seems scarcely to have scratched the surface of the
> African situation.

Perhaps Miss Gordimer spoke up too soon. This volume will show how
far African writers have come within such a short time in defining their
political ideologies. Certainly, not all the writers are as doctrinaire as
Sembene Ousmane. Yet hardly one among them leaves his readers in
doubt about the political fate that he proposes for his society.

'Politics in a work of literature', Stendhal once said, 'is like a pistol-
shot in the middle of a concert, something loud and vulgar, and yet a
thing which it is not possible to refuse one's attention.' Within the past
two decades, no African writer could be found who would agree with this
credo. But Stendhal was not alone in believing that writers should leave
politics alone and embark on the more exalted pursuits of life. 'I am not
interested in politics, I'm interested in style', James Joyce is reputed to

have told his brother Stanilas who had just fled from Italy and was recounting to the novelist the horrors of Mussolini and fascism in Italy. The ultimate justification for this collection of essays lies not in the political views of the writers but in the remarkable variety of methods with which they have interpreted contemporary realities and proposed their own visions of the future. Yet, here too, it is possible to discern an underlying unity. Even when employing a mode as 'alien' as the novel, African writers have increasingly tried to indigenize not only the language but also the form of their art. They no longer address themselves to a foreign audience, but have dealt with the basic problems that confront Africa; more than that, they have addressed Africans in African voices.

Indeed, each writer must finally be judged by how successful he has been in carrying over his message to his people. Virginia Woolf once wrote: 'Any method is right, every method is right, that expresses what we wish to express, if we are writers; that brings us closer to the novelist's intention if we are readers.' But, as Miss Woolf also added, it is a mistake for a reader to stand outside a book and examine methods.

A word or two about the scope of this collection. The volume is limited to West African literature in order to give each essay more depth than would have been possible if an attempt had been made to cover the whole continent. It was more difficult not to focus even more narrowly by treating, for example, Nigerian writing after the Civil War. In a way remarkably similar to what obtained with the Southern writers after the American Civil War, Nigerian writers now have a deeper inburnt knowledge of the world. An attempt has been made to include as many major works as possible from all over West Africa. But, of course, it is impossible to include every one. A significant omission is Ayi Kwei Armah's *The Beautyful Ones Are Not Yet Born* which burst on the African literary scene in 1968. The volume of commentary on the novel within ten years of its first appearance is an indication of both the novel's high quality and its profound impact. None of Armah's following three novels can stand comparison with his first. Another painful omission is Mongo Beti's latest novels, *Remember Ruben* and *Perpétue*, both published in 1974, and acclaimed excellent works. The essay on another Cameroonian writer in exile, Francis Bebey, will show the experimentation that is going on in Cameroonian writing. From the Ivory Coast, a country which has not featured prominently in African literary circles, comes Ahmadou Kourouma's *Les Soleils des Indépendances*, one of the best novels to appear from francophone West Africa.

The contributors to this collection were given only one guideline: to concentrate attention upon the works themselves. It was hoped that they would thereby avoid any overt attempt to define their theoretical positions as critics. But there is no doubt that such definitions are implicit in all the essays. This is a book of responses, of appreciations and of judgements – not of demonstrations.

1
Wole Soyinka and the Novelist's Responsibility in Africa

▼▼▼▼▼▼▼▼▼▼▼▼▼▼▼▼▼▼▼▼▼▼▼▼▼▼▼▼▼▼

KOLAWOLE OGUNGBESAN

'THAT book is good in vain, which the reader throws away', Dr Samuel Johnson once warned. This warning applies perhaps more to the novelist than to any other writer. And among African novelists Wole Soyinka best exemplifies the truth and the moral of Dr Johnson's warning. African writers in general do not believe that they should abdicate their ethical role by eliminating themselves, and therefore the question of responsibility to their readers, from their books. They value the relation of writer to reader and take very seriously their moral obligation to their audience. This essay intends to examine Soyinka's conception of the writer's responsibility, how his novels have been affected by it, how it affects his reputation with his readers and how it is related to his current intellectual position.

When Soyinka's first novel, *The Interpreters*, was published in 1965, practically all the early reviews were favourable, and some were downright adulatory. But critical opinion quickly settled against the novel, and although it is still sometimes mentioned it is hardly read, even in the universities. How is one to explain this sudden decline in the fortune of a book which was once proclaimed as the African novel of the future? Virtually all the participants at a symposium on 'The novel and reality in Africa and America', in Lagos in 1973, seemed to have agreed with Michael Echeruo that it was because Soyinka did not respond to the climate of opinion around him. 'Nobody is bothered, I am afraid, by *The Interpreters*', Echeruo scorned. 'It has not disturbed anybody as far as I know. It does not address itself to a general emotion.'[1]

The round condemnation of his novel by Nigerian scholars would particularly pain Soyinka because he has always stressed the importance of indigenous critics in the development of a literature. In 1962, when he had not published even a single play, Soyinka said that the greatest handicap to the development of Nigerian writing was the lack of a 'really fearless but very honest and intelligent critical forum'. Criticism is so important, he went on, because 'a critic's job is not merely to review an existing piece of work but also to create an atmosphere of appreciation, of tolerance; to cultivate an experimental attitude not only in writers but in the audience'. He condemned critics who pander to the laziness of the audience by supporting the latter's 'instincts to reject what seems strange'.[2]

It is as if Soyinka was trying to prepare the ground for the reception of his first novel which, he claimed during the interview, would be published in the following year. When *The Interpreters* finally came out, three years later, it struck everyone as markedly different from the preceding African novels all of which Soyinka had condemned as writing which aimed to 'bring a closer understanding of Africa to the outside world'. He had stressed, instead, the necessity to build 'responses primarily to the individual work of art'. He continued: 'This attitude needs no pleas other than the truism of individual direction of the creative impulse.'[3] The belief that a writer must, first of all, be true to himself, that he must be independent and original, is the core of Soyinka's view of the artist as one who draws his vision from experience, which begins with self-knowledge. All the same, Soyinka was fully aware of the 'external responsibility'[4] of the novelist. He would agree with Achebe that the writer's duty is 'to explore in depth the human condition. In Africa he cannot perform this task unless he has a proper sense of history.'[5] But Soyinka felt that Achebe, by dwelling so nostalgically on the past, was robbing himself of the opportunity to perform the more urgent task for his society, the projection of a future society. 'The time has now come', Soyinka told a gathering of African writers in 1967, 'when the African writer must have the courage to determine what alone can be salvaged from the recurrent cycle of human stupidity.'[6] How best can the writer do this? Soyinka went on:

> It is about time that the African writer stopped being a mere chronicler and understood also that part of his essential purpose is to write with a very definite vision . . . he must at least begin by exposing the future in a clear and truthful exposition of the present.[7]

The Interpreters attempts to maintain a proper historic viewpoint. Egbo, the most 'authorial' character, is most intimately connected with the past because of the choice he has to make between taking over the inheritance of his father's kingdom in the delta or becoming a bureaucrat in Lagos. Instead of being nostalgic, he is resentful of his traditional past, as he complains to Bandele and Sekoni: 'If the dead are not strong enough to be ever-present in our being, should they not be as they are, dead?'[8] When Sekoni replies that to make such distinctions would disrupt the dome of continuity, which is what life is, Egbo acknowledges that the past cannot be ignored, although it is tempting to do so, for 'the present, equally futile, distinguishes itself only by a particularly abject lack of courage' (p. 121). So, where would morality come from? Egbo replies firmly: 'A man's gift of life should be separate, an unrelated thing. All choice must come from within him, not from promptings of his past' (p. 120).

The contemporary reality which Soyinka dealt with in *The Interpreters* was highlighted in a paper on 'Modern black African theatre', which he delivered at the First World Festival of Negro Arts in Dakar in 1966. The paper, subtitled 'The Nigerian scene, a study of tyranny and individual suppression', sums up the first five years of Nigerian political independence, 1960 to 1965:

> The trial undergone by the individual has taken on a new intensity. It has been more disruptive than under colonial rule for internal strife has brought with it the shattering effect of brother betraying brother and the revolt of men of the same blood. With intellectuals the case of the individual conscience has taken on tragic dimensions.[9]

The Interpreters deals with the problems of the intellectuals in the emerging African nations, a question of individual sensibility at war with the claims of society. The interpreters, the novel's composite 'hero', are young intellectuals all of whom have had their visions frustrated by their society.

Soyinka was not the first Nigerian novelist to present the emerging African élite at war with its society. Achebe, to cite just one example, had treated this theme in his second novel, *No Longer at Ease* (1960). But the view of this conflict presented in *The Interpreters* was revolutionary in Nigerian fiction in 1965. Unlike the protagonists of earlier novels, the interpreters are strong enough to contain to a large extent the influence of society upon themselves. True, each of them is afraid of failure in case he proves inadequate in controlling himself; but each also confronts his fear with courage and determination. And in spite of the pain caused by their determination to master their own destinies, they pursue their ways relentlessly. To defeat the contemporary absurd society the individual needs to be adequate. When Egbo asks a female university student 'Who dares to be adequate?', she replies firmly, 'One can be. It is necessary to be' (p. 134). In this sense, *The Interpreters* is an optimistic book, for it says definitely that, with courage and determination, the individual can effect change and improvement, in himself and consequently in his society. 'I don't believe that I have any obligation to enlighten, to instruct, to teach', Soyinka said in 1962. 'I don't possess that sense of duty or didacticism.'[10] Indeed, his purpose in *The Interpreters* is to explain the *status quo*, not to advocate ways of changing it. By calling his central characters 'the interpreters' Soyinka is emphasizing that their role is to analyse their society, not re-create it. The motto of Sagoe's Voidante Philosophy – 'To shit is human, to voidate divine' – explains the delusions which society has created instead of facing the truth about itself. The Voidant Philosophy is a means of forcing society to acknowledge the disgusting and embarrassing values by which it lives. This is illustrated in the incident of the night-soil van accident. 'Over twenty yards were spread huge pottage mounds, twenty yards of solid and running, plebeian and politician, indigenous and foreign shit. Right on the tarred road' (p. 108). Everyone has contributed to the shit, yet everyone ignores it – including the newspapers, all of which believe that publishing articles or pictures of the affected area would offend their readers. Yet after five days the shit has not been removed – although it raises a stench that cannot be ignored. Voidancy is an attempt to cope with such mass self-deception.

Soyinka, by analysing the prevalent mood, aimed to force society to recognize the true nature of its problems. Such recognition would be an indispensable step towards solving the problems. Here, Soyinka's conception of the writer's duty to his society is remarkably similar to that of the nineteenth-century European novelists with their exclusive concern for understanding their societies. Their novels show an obsession with 'interpreting' the nature of an absurd society. However, it is because Soyinka interpreted the novelist's duty in such conservative terms that *The Interpreters* has proved most inadequate to more revolutionary African writers. Nadine Gordimer, the white South African novelist, finds that, in spite of its perceptive analysis of society, *The Interpreters* 'does not suggest a reordering of society in *political* terms as a possible solution'.[11] She therefore lumps the novel with all African fiction of the 1960s in which she finds little indication that the political fate seeks to determine itself in terms of profound social change. And Ngugi wa Thiong'o has more strongly criticized Soyinka for neglecting in *The Interpreters* 'the creative struggle of the masses' by not involving his characters in the dialectics of struggle:

> It is not enough for the African artist, standing aloof, to view society and highlight its weaknesses. He must try to go beyond this, to seek

out the sources, the causes and the trends of a revolutionary struggle which has already destroyed the traditional power-map drawn up by the colonialist nations.[12]

'If the writer feels committed or involved', Soyinka said in 1967, 'or if he feels a compulsion within himself to write the truth, then he surely has the right to try and build the kind of society in which he can write this beautiful literature, these beautiful words.'[13] What Soyinka was talking about is the writer engaging in direct political action, not his providing an ideological vision in a work of art. However, the political crisis in Nigeria between 1967 and 1970 forced Soyinka to become more intimately involved in politics. As a result he was detained by the Nigerian government in 1967. Soon after his release in 1969, he went into exile. Detention revolutionized Soyinka's view of literature as a political weapon. True, he claimed to remain convinced that the writer should be committed to the restoration of 'the permanent values – justice, freedom, human dignity' in his society. But he also admitted that he recognized the 'impotence' of literature in performing this function:

> The exercise of the literary function may serve the writer – and perhaps a few followers – to keep in view what the ends of humanity are. They may eventually be spurred to action in defence of those ends. In our own society especially it is essential to recognize this. At the moment literature and art can only function as a KEEP-IN-VIEW tray on a bureaucrat's desk. Once this is accepted, the writer does not fool himself into thinking that all is said and all is done that need be said and done. He holds himself in readiness – accelerating the process where he can – when the minutes in that file can be made a live project. No other attitude seems possible to me.[14]

In contrast, Soyinka looked up to his prison notes, *The Man Died*, to accomplish the revolution he had in view. 'In a very crucial way the book is a test of the people themselves', he affirmed; 'it is a test of those who claim to think on behalf of the people and a gauge of the potential for the only kind of political action which I foresee – with no alternatives.'[15]

Season of Anomy reflects Soyinka's new awareness of the writer's responsibility within the increasing pace of social change taking place in his society. In 1967, he had said: 'When the writer in his society can no longer function as conscience, he must recognize that his choice lies between denying himself totally or withdrawing to the position of chronicler and post-mortem surgeon.'[16] In 1972, Soyinka moved from being merely the conscience of his society to being a political revolutionary. The form of *Season of Anomy*, like that of *The Man Died*, is determined by his stated objective 'of effecting the revolutionary changes to which I have become more than ever dedicated'.[17] How revolutionary *Season of Anomy* is in comparison with *The Interpreters* can be easily demonstrated on the level of characterization. Although in *The Interpreters* a group of characters had occupied the stage, the most 'authorial' of them was Egbo (he is painted as Ogun, Soyinka's favourite god in the pantheon). In *Season of Anomy* Ofeyi is modelled after Egbo – in fact the author once mistakenly calls him Egbo.[18] Egbo's dilemma whether to inherit his grandfather's chiefdom or take up a job in Lagos is re-enacted in Ofeyi's dilemma whether to accept the leadership of the Aiyero people or go off on his more private quest of Iriyise. Ofeyi, like Egbo, is drawn towards two women – but this theme is used to serve political ends in *Season of Anomy*. Union with Taiila who had intended to become a nun would make Ofeyi renounce public commitment in search of spiritual peace; in artistic terms this would mean his forsaking the demands of a committed writer, living for himself and his art. However, by braving all dangers to rescue Iriyise, the symbol of the potential beauty of the society, from the clutches of the reactionary forces in Cross-River, Ofeyi reaffirms the writer's commitment to rescue for his people their beautiful destiny.

   Season of Anomy, unlike *The Interpreters*, is truly a political novel. It analyses political motives, actions and their consequences. However, because it deals with the world of action, where ideas as well as personalities become both polarized and simplified, it is inevitably less complex than *The Interpreters*. Clearly Soyinka means to subjugate art to social purpose. Here, he carries the war to his enemies. For, it is Ofeyi who imbues the men of Aiyero (who constitute the progressive forces in the story) with his revolutionary ideas, and thereby initiates the fight against the Cartel, which later provokes the massacre from the reactionary forces. But soon Ofeyi is forced to yield leadership of the progressive forces to the Dentist (Demakin), the apostle of violence whose morality is summed up by the professional ethics to extract the tooth of evil before it infects others. True, Ofeyi himself is not averse to violence. But the Dentist, the 'selective assassinator', goes beyond Ofeyi's stated objective, the 'need to protect the young seedling' (p. 23) of the revolution, and justifies the use of violence as a means of seizing the initiative from the Cartel whose more efficient system of creating violence threatens to annihilate the Aiyero ideal. As the full dimension of the wanton destruction wrought by the Cartel becomes known he wrests from Ofeyi the task of leading Aiyero against the Cartel. Indeed, it is only through his intervention that Iriyise and Ofeyi himself are able to escape from Cross-River.

Has the novelist, in this apparent glorification of violence, not lost sight of his major function, to project a future which will redeem, not brutalize, the mass of the people? Answering in the affirmative, Femi Osofisan, one of Nigeria's youngest novelists, claims in his essay on 'Chaos and political vision in recent literature', that Soyinka's 'post-independence disillusionment has reached the second stage, which is cynicism'. For, according to Osofisan, it is only a novelist whose vision has palled that can make the Dentist, the disciple of violence and political assassination, triumphant, the man to shape our social destiny.[19] However, it must be stressed that Soyinka accepts violence, not for its own sake, but as an indispensable ingredient in the struggle. In *Season of Anomy*, it is only a weapon, clearly subjugated to the social vision on behalf of which it is employed. Ofeyi and Demakin are indeed the two facets – the creative and the destructive, respectively – of 'the comprehensive Ogunnian personality'. The Dentist is the man of the hour. In the 'season of anomy', violence becomes an inevitable prelude to political emancipation. But it remains only a means, to be used to achieve that higher ideal which it is the business of the man of vision to define. The Dentist himself acknowledges as much to Ofeyi: 'Don't ask me what I envisage. Beyond the elimination of men I know to be destructively evil, I envisage nothing. What happens after is up to people like you' (p. 112).

Soyinka's aim is to evoke a new society in the process of coming to birth. In making Ofeyi (Orpheus) successfully rescue Iriyise (Eurydice) from Cross-River (Hades), Soyinka violates his allegorical source, because he can see only one resolution to the conflict in his society. 'The goals were clear enough,' Ofeyi tells Pa Ahime, 'the dream a new concept of labouring hands across artificial frontiers, the concrete, affective presence of Aiyero throughout the land, undermining the Cartel's superstructure of robbery, indignities and murder, ending the new phase of slavery' (p. 27). And if, as some critics have complained, Ofeyi does not adequately articulate his vision, it is because Soyinka wants to prevent the rhetorical intrusion of his ideology. Instead, as the structure of the novel shows very clearly, he makes it organic to the process of the birth of a new society.

Soyinka as a novelist deserves to be taken seriously because of his high intellectual position among African writers. A speculative thinker, his persistent call to African writers to demonstrate that they have a vision shows that he sees the literary artist as a redeemer. He believes that the writer possesses an inner light unavailable to the mass of his people, and that it is his duty to use this inspiration and insight to guide his society towards a beautiful future. As he said in 1967, 'the question of a vision simply refers to the contribution of the writer to the kind of human society – individual, parochial or world – that he believes in'.[20] However, it is the obscurity of his work, rather than his belief that it is not the writer's duty to teach, that has failed to recommend Soyinka to his Nigerian audience which, as Achebe pointed out, is only too eager for guidance from its writers. Indeed, Soyinka's refusal to tone down his language to the assimilative capacity of his audience has led Nigerian critics to query the social relevance of his works. One of them, concluding a particularly severe criticism of Soyinka as a novelist, wrote: 'Any work of fiction or poetry whose words are too obscure for the so-called simple, but literate, audience is not suitable for human consumption, except, perhaps, as a riddle.'[21] Another, in his contribution to the symposium on 'The novel and reality in Africa and America', called *The Interpreters* a failure because 'it does not belong to the society'.[22]

In contrast, Soyinka has ridiculed writers who simplify their language in order to condition social consciousness: 'the energy and passion of social revolution appears perversely to quarry into the metaphorical resources of language in order to brand its message deeper in the heart of humanity'.[23] He has continued to claim that he does not think of any audience when he writes. Although his novels deal with the most profound experiences of his society, they have been condemned by Nigerian critics as hardly relevant to that society. In return, Soyinka dismisses all Nigerian critics as 'very simple ostriches – with their heads buried in quicksands. We must give them up for lost and await the hatching of new eggs.'[24] His defiant justification of the obscurity of his work means that he does not want to be understood at the cost of trimming down his meaning to the assimilative capacity of simple minds. In what he considers the complacent literary culture of contemporary Nigeria, Soyinka does not even acknowledge that there may be an effective minority of readers who may understand and value his work.

In spite of the artistic faults in his books, Soyinka deserves recognition as a novelist. The kind of imaginative technique which he employed in *The Interpreters* was new in the African novel – and it has remained rare. He was most naturally inclined to drama; and it is obvious that a dramatic mind is at work in both *The Interpreters* and *Season of Anomy*. Soyinka, poet and dramatist, sometimes fails in transposing his talent to the narrative mode. His novels contain both lyric and dramatic elements which have not been fully integrated into the longer genre.

Concluding a defence of *Season of Anomy* against reviewers who complained that it was difficult to grasp what was going on or what Soyinka was driving at, a critic made a point which also applies to *The Interpreters*: 'But the novel *does* work and read effectively at the narrative level; it is, to put it crudely, a compulsive read for much of its length.'[25] A novel must indeed 'work' if it is to be a great one; but it is not a machine, and value can exist in one which, strictly, fails. A first-hand understanding and sympathetic appreciation of Soyinka's novels seems indispensable to any serious reader of African fiction.

References

1. Theo Vincent (ed.), *The Novel and Reality in Africa and America* (Lagos, 1973), p. 26.
2. Dennis Duerden and Cosmo Pieterse (eds.), *African Writers Talking* (London, Heinemann, 1972) pp. 176–7.
3. Wole Soyinka, 'Nigeria's International Film Festival, 1962', *Nigeria Magazine*, LXXIX (December 1963), p. 309.
4. Wole Soyinka, 'And after the Narcissist?', *African Forum*, I, 4 (Spring 1966), p. 54.
5. Chinua Achebe, 'The role of the writer in a new nation', in Douglas Killam (ed.), *African Writers on African Writing* (London, Heinemann, 1973), p. 8.
6. Wole Soyinka, 'The writer in a modern Africa state', in Per Wastberg (ed.), *The Writer in Modern Africa* (Uppsala, Scandinavian Institute of African Studies, 1968), p. 20.
7. ibid., p. 58.
8. Wole Soyinka, *The Interpreters* (London, Heinemann, 1965), p. 9. Further references to the novel will be inserted in the essay.
9. Wole Soyinka, 'Le théâtre moderne négro-africain', Première Festival mondial des arts nègres, Dakar, 1–24 avril 1966, *Colloque sur l'art nègre: Rapport*, Tome 1 (Paris, Société africaine de culture, 1967), pp. 547–8.
10. Duerden and Pieterse, op. cit., p. 173.
11. Nadine Gordimer, *The Black Interpreters: Notes on African Writing* (Johannesburg, Raven Press, 1973), p. 44.
12. Ngugi wa Thiong'o, 'Wole Soyinka, T. M. Aluko and the satiric voice', in *Homecoming* (London, Heinemann, 1972), pp. 65–6.
13. Wastberg, op. cit., p. 52.
14. Interview by Biodun Jeyifous, *Transition*, 42 (1973), p. 62.
15. ibid., p. 63.
16. Wastberg, op. cit., p. 21.
17. Wole Soyinka, *The Man Died* (London, Rex Collings, 1972), p. 15.
18. Wole Soyinka, *Season of Anomy* (London, Rex Collings, 1973), p. 152. Further references to the novel will be inserted in the essay.
19. Femi Osofisan, 'Anubis resurgent: chaos and political vision in recent literature', *Ch'indaba*, 2 (July/December 1976), p. 47.
20. Wastberg, op. cit., p. 52.
21. O. O. Enekwe, 'Wole Soyinka as a novelist', *Okike*, (1975), p. 76.
22. Vincent, op. cit., p. 28.
23. Wole Soyinka, *Myth, Literature and the African World* (London, Cambridge University Press, 1976), p. 63.
24. *Transition*, 42, p. 64.
25. E. Wright, in *African Literature Today*, 8 (1976), p. 117.

2
The Nigerian Crisis in the Nigerian Novel

▼▼▼▼▼▼▼▼▼▼▼▼▼▼▼▼▼▼▼▼▼▼▼▼▼▼▼▼

OLALERE OLADITAN

THE major events of 'the Nigerian crisis' are well known: the military coup of 15 January 1966, the mass killing of the Ibos in the northern region, followed by another coup in July of the same year; the creation of states in the following year and the secessionist attempt which culminated in the thirty-month Civil War which ended in January 1970. However the explanations for this cluster of events went further back beyond January 1966 and the consequences continued beyond the cessation of hostilities. The first military eruption hardly makes sense by itself without reckoning with the pervasive politics of graft and violence during the First Republic, the western Nigerian crisis of 1962, the 1964 federal elections, and the troubles in the west up to the eve of the military intervention. The crisis should also include the bloodless coup which swept General Gowon from office in July 1975, and the abortive coup of 13 February 1976 in which General Murtala Muhammed was killed. Furthermore, one cannot honestly dismiss from the crisis the 'oil boom' and its effects: the conspicuous extravagance, corruption and indiscipline which largely explain, and have been used to justify, the spate of coups.

Literary imagination is not bound by factual 'accuracy'; it may deliberately confuse, distort, invent and even falsify. African writers, particularly the novelists, have consistently exercised these poetic liberties over the collective experience of their society in a rich, skilful and purposeful manner. In the case of the Nigerian novelists and the Nigerian crisis, one is immediately struck by the quantity of production and the variety of approach to what is essentially the same subject-matter. After Achebe's pioneering *A Man of the People* (1966), there appeared, among others, Kole Omotoso's *The Combat* (1972) and Wole Soyinka's *Season of Anomy*

(1973), which should be read with his prison notes *The Man Died*, published the previous year. Still in 1973 appeared John Munonye's *A Wreath for the Maidens* and Elechi Amadi's *Sunset in Biafra*, and Samuel U. Ifejika's *The New Religion*. Since then, Femi Osofisan's *Kolera Kolej* (1975) and Chukwuemeka Ike's *Sunset at Dawn* (1976) have been published.

This essay attempts to classify all these samples according to the approaches to, and the uses made of, the political crisis. The grouping done here is only provisional. Firstly, numerous as the works considered may appear, not all the novels treating the period of the crisis have been examined; more works continue to be produced and some of the published ones are not yet readily available. However, it is hoped that one may be able to classify the others along the lines adopted here. Secondly, this study is tentative because only the most striking features are emphasized in every case and it is on the basis of these few qualities that works have been grouped together. Definitely, more characteristics can be identified in each work and one can set up other forms of resemblances as criteria for establishing other 'types'.

The first *coup d'état* in 1966 was a fulfilment of the prognostics at the end of *A Man of the People*. The novel describes political corruption after independence and ends with a coup in which the military men take over the reins of government and ban all partisan politics. Written between 1964 and 1965, and published early in 1966, it is a prophecy which finds immediate fulfilment. The corruption, graft and cynicism in Nigeria must have led Achebe to conclude that Nigeria too was ripe for her own share of the military takeovers sweeping through the continent. But soon after January 1966 Nigerians discovered that 'Nangaism' or political corruption is not the preserve of self-professed politicians; the military, too, can turn Nanga. As if to re-emphasize the initial futuristic significance of his work, Achebe declared in 1974:

> *A Man of the People* has often been described as a story of the corruption of politicians. I prefer to see it as a novel of political corruption. I featured politicians in it because they were handy in 1964–65 when the book was written. If I wrote it today the *dramatis personnae* in all likelihood would be in uniform.[1]

John Munonye's *A Wreath for the Maidens*[2] and Chukwuemeka Ike's *Sunset at Dawn*[3] deal no longer with forecasts but with witnesses to and records of events. Munonye summarizes the major political events in Nigeria from the last days of colonial rule to the latter part of the Civil War soon after the fall of Port Harcourt. Ike's novel is wholly set in the Civil War, opening with the beginning of the Biafran adventure after

Aburi and ending with the formal surrender after the secessionist leaders' escape to the Ivory Coast. Both works are replete with recognizable historical events, but neither is a faithful record of the crisis. For example, both novels attain a cover-up in the choice and naming of the characters. Historical personages are hardly mentioned by their real names, even in the obvious case of the secessionist leader, Colonel Ojukwu. He is simply referred to as H.E. (His Excellency) in Ike's work and, in Munonye's work the closest figure to him is Major (and later Colonel) Nzellia who is later reassigned to become the principal co-ordinator of the Civilian Corps, 'a duty as nebulous in name as it was in its scope'. Some of the other characters are types rather than specific historical figures. Munonye's Eduado Boga, like Achebe's Nanga, embodies the corruption of the pre-coup era, while the narrators Ekonte Biere and Roland Medo exemplify critical opinions within the breakaway enclave. Similarly, Ike's hero, Dr Kanu, is the faithful nationalist, committed first to the Nigerian cause and later to Biafra, but remaining throughout loyal, selfless and somewhat naive in his pursuit of the nation's interest.

The two novels are imbued with a strong humanistic concern. Munonye's work bears an indelible moral imprint which is sustained by the heroes and narrators. Although these itinerant witnesses are ready to participate in the actions when invited, they stand out of the common run of political leadership and remain at that remove of objectivity which allows for a critical analysis of the successive events and a just assessment of the other actors. They raise the moral and political questions at the heart of the crisis and blame everything on the greed and corruption of the leaders who make the common people their victims both before and during the war. Their subsequent appointments into the secessionist state's government provide an ample chance to express these views courageously to the highest authorities. Outwitted by the 'moderates' and the crooks, they soon become mere outcasts dreaming of that day when justice will triumph and the common man will be avenged.

In *Sunset at Dawn*, in spite of the relatively enlivened presentation of the crisis, an unmistakable reflective tone is attained through the detailed and pathetic picture of suffering, violence and carnage coupled with the cruel irony of fate, all heightened by the focus on Dr Kanu's family. It is particularly ironic that the very people symbolic of Nigerian unity – Fatima, Ami junior, Halima and her child – suffer most and make the highest sacrifices. Although the faith, dedication, enthusiasm and commitment of most Biafrans – soldiers and civilians alike – are not in doubt, God seems to be fighting on the side of the bigger and superior battalions, those of Nigeria. Because the 'Rising Sun', the Biafran emblem, also suggests a sunset, the nation's death is contained in its birth, and the overall image at the end of the novel is that of a giant human structure smothered at its proud beginning: the sun, indeed, set in the early hours of dawn.

An equally tragic equivocation underlies Elechi Amadi's *Sunset in Biafra*,[4] which, with Wole Soyinka's *The Man Died*,[5] do not strictly qualify as fiction. The latter contains Soyinka's own prison notes. Amadi's story, subtitled 'A Civil War Diary', is described in the Foreword as 'an intimate, personal story, told for its own sake'. The two books have attracted the attention of literary critics partly because their authors were already proven creative writers but also because their own artistic merits recommend them for consideration alongside literary works. Furthermore, in the context of this essay, they bear a significant and distinctive relationship to the Nigerian crisis.

Amadi's perspective is different from Ike's in *Sunset at Dawn*, although the two authors focus on happenings in the secessionist area. In contrast to the loyal Biafran in Ike's novel, Amadi's diary records the experiences of a conscientious objector who is subjected to arbitary arrests, and detention under deplorable conditions. On the whole, the cursory and episodic treatment of events in *A Wreath* and *Sunset at Dawn* is particularized in *Sunset in Biafra*, and Amadi's 'true story' lends greater credibility to the fictionalized efforts of Ike and Munonye. Soyinka's is another true story but set this time in the quieter parts of the nation in crisis. Like Amadi, he relates the role of a critical intellectual and the woes of detention, this time on the federal side, at more numerous places and over a longer period. The problems facing the two detainees are largely the same: harassment, endless and mainly stereotyped interrogations, moments of hope and pitfalls of frustration, danger of death and the battle for self-preservation. Both victims also raise the moral and political issues of the crisis, but they contrast sharply in their attitudes to their ordeals and in the tones employed in their records. Amadi, even in his bitterest moment, is restrained, although his forthrightness sometimes borders on naivety. He aspires to, and often attains, objectivity in the presentation of his role, setting out the arguments of the various sides, almost to the point of being too expository and at times apologetic. Finally, his narrative is characterized by the smoothness, directness and simplicity of his first novel, *The Concubine* (1966).

The qualities of Soyinka's document are to be sought in regions other than these. Against Amadi's strong factual basis is what has been termed Soyinka's 'general lack of concreteness' in political details.[6] Whereas

Amadi is constantly engaged in a cool assessment of situations, seeking expedient solutions and sometimes assenting to compromises, Soyinka maintains an ethical absolutism and remains suspicious and alert in all his dealings with his captors. Survival for him lies not in a quiet opposition of reason to power but in reciprocated intimidation and blackmail achieved through hungerstrike, agitation (even in detention) and in the establishment of breaches in the thick wall of his enemy's security. Intellectual engagement is the essence of Soyinka's occupation in solitary confinement, particularly in Kaduna, but this serves not only to safeguard his personal survival but also to emphasize his superiority to his captors. Every withdrawal into the deeper self is followed by a round of demential explosion which comes in devastating verbal outpourings and great poetic flights. Indeed, *The Man Died* readily satisfies Soyinka's own comparison of a book to 'a hammer, a hand grenade which you detonate under a stagnant way of looking at the world'.[7]

The Man Died and *Sunset in Biafra* predictably treat events, places and personages who bear immediate political relevance to the Nigerian crisis. But Soyinka adopts a more personal note than Amadi. His ability to evoke a whole atmosphere rather than relate all the facts, as well as his tendency to disguise or merely hint at subjects in which the reader's interest is already aroused (a Third Force, the new north, ideology for the country), invests his narrative with that absorbing touch which carries reality to the vague and broad precincts of fiction, and lifts his tirade to the level of a passionate plea for the protection of a people against the profiteers and prostitutes of power. Personal vengeance translates into a commitment to justice, not only for a specific society but also for humanity at large, and assumes some ideological dimension in the novel which issued from the same context and inspiration.

The primary questions in *Season of Anomy*[8] relate to the roles of ideology and violence in a revolutionary transformation of society. Soyinka attempts to draw a redemptive meaning from the chaos, violence and destruction that have attended his country's recent past. Some of the material for the novel derives from the experience related in *The Man Died*, particularly the northern riots and the massacres in which the author was caught during a hazardous visit. Soyinka invests the novel with the predominant characteristics of the Nigerian crisis: confusion, disorder and violence. Indeed, to obtain a coherent story in *Season of Anomy* the reader is obliged to impose order on the confusion, and this is only rarely fully attained after a great expenditure of mental effort directed at the comprehension and reconstruction of both the text and the crisis. Ofeyi, the protagonist and renegade sales promoter for the

Cocoa Cartel, sees in Aiyero an ideal society, particularly for the propagation of his ideology. As soon as Pa Ahime cedes the young people of this island who are already widely scattered all over the land to Ofeyi, the latter makes them his evangelists in Cross-River, a Muslim part of the country where the natives of Aiyero are regarded as 'alien' workers. The Cartel abruptly starts a campaign of harassment and massacre against these aliens in Cross-River and it is during the ensuing chaos that Iriyise, Ofeyi's girlfriend, is abducted in the course of a performance tour of the beleaguered area with Zaccheus's band. Afterwards, the focus shifts to the orphic search for the loved and lost one.

The inconclusiveness and elusiveness of *The Man Died* recur here, particularly on the central issues of the novel – the redemption of a lost society and the means of that retrieval: ideology or violence, force and blood, or reason alone. The ideology is poorly defined by the ideologue himself although there are indications that it probably has to do with some form of communism, for its goals are presented as a fulfilment of 'the dream of labouring hands across artificial frontiers, the concrete, affective presence of Aiyero throughout the land, undermining the Cartel's superstructure of robbery, indignities and murder, ending the new phase of slavery' (p. 27). The Marxian call upon all the workers of the world is echoed here, and the Cartel in the novel is indeed a capitalist body. But the discussion of this ideal is intermittent and inconclusive. After the abduction of Iriyise all we hear of the ideology is the argument between Ofeyi and Demakin, the Dentist, on the relative merits of violence and reason in any serious effort to change society. Pa Ahime, that lucid tutor so crucial and so impressive in the first section, is dropped for the rescue of the girl, although this is not necessarily a selfish quest displacing a more glorious pursuit of a common and public good: it re-enacts that hazardous trip taken by Soyinka himself to the eastern region in quest of a resolution of the Nigerian conflict. Elevated by the concern for justice in *The Man Died* and the suggestive name of Ofeyi (Orpheus, Orphée), the individual quest in *Season of Anomy* symbolizes the community's descent to hell to recapture the good and the beautiful.

However, it is the character of Demakin, the Dentist, that apologist of violence, that imposes itself at the end of the novel. Only his ruthlessness and cunning can rescue Ofeyi and Iriyise and thus guarantee the success of the mission, be it at its immediate personal level or in its wider societal symbolization. If this is not a definite choice, which has been condemned,[9] it is at least a recognition of the relevance and effectiveness of violence at a certain moment. The suggestion here is that the acceptance of this weapon is a matter of maturity and responsibility.

In Samuel Ifejika's *The New Religion*[10] the focus shifts from politics and the violent events of the Civil War to the subtle yet traumatic economic, socio-moral and psychological dimension of the troubled period. Ifejika's work is a critique of the postwar Nigerian society's 'new religion' of quick money, an obsessive materialism which Dr Onochie personifies. This 'war case' personality is a victim of civil service red-tapism. Onochie qualified abroad as a veterinary doctor before the war, and returns to his old place of work but the bureaucrats do not regularize his appointment in line with his new and higher qualification. He is therefore condemned to the status and remuneration of a School Certificate holder. This deprivation initially explains the hero's moral degeneration. He becomes a gambler and a liar. Even when some wealth offers an opportunity for self-retrieval, he remains morally bankrupt, indulging in women, debauchery and extravagance. His taste for money soon becomes a mania. At the outbreak of a cholera epidemic he steals animal drugs to use on the villagers, but the law finally catches up with him.

As Ifejika himself states in his note to the novel, many of the characters, particularly the 'educated' ones, are 'representative types' in contemporary African society. These characters lack the moral strength to withstand the socio-economic stresses of the crisis-ridden society; their fall is particularly distressing since they are 'people expected to know better'. They include Professor Ikemba who uses his position on the University Tenders Board to enrich himself, his immediate relatives and friends. Ifejika is, however, a confident social idealist and his novel manifests what has been termed 'interventionism': the author expressly demands (and portrays) positive action on the part of the state, organized institutions and private persons to improve social relations.[11] It is hoped that reason and justice will prevail, that certain individuals will be honest, altruistic and disciplined enough to save others and the society at large.

The inventiveness displayed by these novelists on the thematic level is matched by their experiments in form. In *Season of Anomy*, for example, Soyinka adopts effectively the 'revue' mode which belongs primarily to the stage. In *A Wreath for the Maidens* and *Sunset at Dawn*, history and fiction are mixed in different proportions. Indeed, a few novels deserve attention mainly for their stylistic conceptions. They include Kole Omotoso's *The Combat* and Femi Osofisan's *Kolera Kolej*.

The Combat,[12] a symbolic parody of the Civil War, is dedicated to Christopher Okigbo, the Nigerian poet who perished in the war. In the novel, a taxi driver, Chuku Debe, runs over a boy but denies responsibility when challenged by his bosom friend, Ojo Dada, with whom he shares the same room. The combat fixed to resolve the problem soon assumes international proportions and engages the interest of the world press and the super-powers. The parody becomes obvious when the content is related to Nigerian history. The victim was born in 1960, the year of Nigeria's independence; the two friends are from different Nigerian tribes; the contending super-powers, Russia and the United States, wooed Nigeria during the war, an event which excited the interest of the world press. However, in the novel the fratricidal war is constantly reported in the sports' section, representing perhaps the overall attitude behind the foreign interest in the crisis.

There is an undercurrent of tragic awareness in the characters of two friends, who have always regarded themselves as brothers, but now are at loggerheads over a child begotten by a prostitute. The friends are reduced to mere pawns of the East and West; and the source of their calamities is only a big joke to the press and the ideologically divided world. Worse still, the foreign meddlers aspire to being the real benefactors of the fight, bargaining to win the boy and the mother, the real prizes of the duel. This tragic note is heightened by the poem which precedes the last chapters: it emphasizes the immediate relevance of the whole work to the Nigerian national tragedy:

> questions
> what paranoaic wrath drove us thus far
> what rain storms shall come to wash this
>   stream of blood away
> what river floods shall dampen this jungle
>   floor and wipe our guilt away
> make liquid this plastered blood and purge
>   our lives again
> what avatar shall be to lead us to other
>   beginnings?
>
> wherever you rest oh restless rain torrents
>   you bear merely
> the ambergris for this purple dye has stuck
>   fast to us.   (p. 83)

Femi Osofisan in *Kolera Kolej*[13] examines the quality of decolonization in Africa and its consequences on the post-independence situation. Despite this continental perspective, most of the thinly veiled episodes are drawn from Nigeria. A university represents the colonized land; independence is granted for and at the metropolis's convenience: because the college is under the scourge of a cholera epidemic. Furthermore, the departing colonial power enshrines in the Yandi Convention

– a part of the 'independence' protocols – terms which ensure the eternal dependence of the new nation on its old master. The latter controls the economy, dictates the foreign policy, determines the military strength and imposes its language as the official language of the former colony; a colonialist composes the new nation's anthem. Essentially dependent in every sense, the new nation knows no stability. In a way quite suggestive of the Nigerian situation, tribalism, corruption, unrest and violence become the patterns of life; machinations, thuggery, coups and counter-coups become the accepted processes of conflict resolution and, in most cases, the changes in leadership indicate no clear political orientation. This insight into the African political scene is communicated in a very light tone, touching on the burlesque and the farce. Here, various experiences assume the cloak of the absurd, sometimes in the Sartrean sense of the contingent. This part of the opening chapter is typical:

> When the journalists had assembled, in the freshly pruned garden near the Women's Hall, the acting Vice-Chancellor mounted a small rostrum and adjusted his glasses. And it was then that a curious thing happened. The VC was suddenly seen to double up, so suddenly in fact that his chin hit the lectern – and, even before the journalists could record this spectacular manner of beginning a speech, he had straightened up again and just as suddenly, his arms spread out beside him like a bird about to take off. Cameras flashed at once. The VC had definitely invented a novel form of rhetoric.
> And once again, he had done it, bending forward to hit the lectern and straightening up, with the same precision and the same remarkable swiftness. And for a third time. The gathering cheered, incredulous. But at this stage the VC seemed to have reckoned that the performance was getting monotonous, for this time, as he came up again, arms outspread, he added a low growling rumble of undecided decibel from somewhere low down under his academic gown. The journalists recorded fast: the VC had added a subtle variation – he had farted.
> And suddenly, from his mouth and from his anus, strange hot liquids began to gush out, and the VC began to dance violently like an apostle mounted by the spirit.
> The porters and the messengers, I believe, were the first to run for it . . .
>
> (pp. 9–10)

A striking characteristic of *Kolera Kolej* is its structure, particularly the brevity and profusion of chapters, features which are also observable but to a lesser extent in *The Combat*. Osofisan's 113-page novel is broken into 44 chapters, 16 within the first 45 pages which constitute Part One, 25 in Part Two, and 3 in the 7-page Postscript. With an average of less than three pages to a chapter, the critic is inevitably intrigued: a few of the pages are actually blank, some of the chapters are less than a page and the longest ones cover less than four pages. Osofisan's style is non-expansive, relying heavily on suggestive words, phrases and even whole situations. The names of characters like Paramole, Kukute and Agborin (Yoruba words meaning snake, stump and deer respectively) give some hints on the personality and roles of the figures so labelled. Similarly, stock names like Ijebu, Ekiti, and Oyo are given their stereotypical significance: for example, the Oyo man, as the name suggests and as most Yoruba are wont to accept, is slippery, diplomatic, unpredictable and cunning. The Yandi Convention evokes the Yaounde Convention which links a number of African countries with the European Common Market through France; and the trouble in the convocation of the Caucus recalls the experience in the House of Assembly in western Nigeria in 1962. Apart from such references and associations of meanings, parts of the text tend to be cryptic. In the ten-line last chapter, for example, we have hints of another *coup d'état*; and the last sentence reads: 'And above it all, above the clamour, rode the warm, triumphant laughter of a woman.' This probably implies that the final act of violence has brought relief and hope, that this last coup may therefore be different from the earlier ones which were essentially directionless.

The works considered above do not by any means constitute all the novels produced on the Nigerian crisis. But it is hoped that the grouping suggested here will help in appreciating some of the others. Okechukwu Mezu's *Behind the Rising Sun*,[14] for example, may be classified with other fictionalized documentaries like Munonye's *A Wreath* and Ike's *Sunset at Dawn*. In his opening chapters Mezu dwells on Biafra's relationship with the external world, Europe in particular, through the various agents charged with propaganda and the purchase of arms. Similarly, Fola Oyewole's *Reluctant Rebel*[15] will largely go with *The Man Died* and *Sunset in Biafra* as personal accounts, except that it is closer to a historical report. For while Soyinka and Amadi place their persons in the forefront, with all the subjectivity of personal emotions and temperament, the crisis *per se* is the concern of Oyewole. He adopts a cold thematic approach and his book shows less literariness than those of Amadi and Soyinka. None the less, Oyewole's account has more literary merits than N. U. Akpan's *The Struggle for Secession*[16] and R. B. Alade's *The Broken Bridge*,[17] both of which are purely historical documents.

Each of the above works deserves closer examination. It will be interesting to focus on how single events, the *coup d'état*, for example, have been handled. Such a study may give a more intimate knowledge of the bearings of recent Nigerian literature from her recent history. It will also be fruitful to examine the politico-moral positions of the writers *vis-à-vis* the crisis. In such a study, prominence will have to be given to the intellectuals, theoreticians or ideologues who figure in almost all the works of this period. Perhaps an understanding of their personalities will reveal the profound sense and significance which the writers have given to the troubles of their times.

References

1. *New Nigerian,* 28 September 1974.
2. *A Wreath for the Maidens* (London, Heinemann, 1973).
3. *Sunset at Dawn* (London, Collins and Harvill Press, 1976).
4. *Sunset in Biafra* (London, Heinemann, 1973).
5. *The Man Died* (London, Rex Collings, 1972).
6. Abiola Irele, 'The season of a mind: Wole Soyinka and the Nigerian crisis', *Benin Review*, 1 (1974), p. 117.
7. In an interview published in Section III of the pamphlet *When the Man Died: Views, Reviews and Interview on Wole Soyinka's Controversial Book*, edited by John Agetua (Benin City, Midwest Newspaper Corporation, 1975).
8. *Season of Anomy* (London, Rex Collings, 1973). All page references in this essay are to this edition.
9. Femi Osofisan, 'Anubis resurgent: chaos and political vision in recent literature', *Ch'indaba*, 2 (July/December 1976), pp. 44–49.
10. *The New Religion* (London, Rex Collings, 1973).
11. Louis Cazamian, *The Social Novel in England, 1830–1850*, trans. Martin Fido (London, Routledge & Kegan Paul, 1973), p. 8.
12. *The Combat* (London, Heinemann, 1972). All page references in this essay are to this edition.
13. *Kolera Kolej* (Ibadan, New Horn Press, 1975). All page references in this essay are to this edition.
14. *Behind the Rising Sun* (London, Heinemann, 1973).
15. *Reluctant Rebel* (London, Rex Collings, 1975).
16. *The Struggle for Secession 1966–1970* (London, Frank Cass, 1971). A personal account of the Nigerian Civil War by N. U. Akpan, the chief secretary to the government and head of service of eastern Nigeria, which declared itself 'Biafra' in 1967.
17. *The Broken Bridge: Reflections and Experiences of a Medical Doctor during the Nigerian Civil War* (Ibadan, Caxton Press, 1975).

3
Ola Rotimi's
Search for a Technique

▼▼▼▼▼▼▼▼▼▼▼▼▼▼▼▼▼▼▼▼▼▼▼▼▼▼

AKANJI NASIRU

A RADICAL shift in emphasis is observable in the works of recent Nigerian dramatists of English expression. Like their counterparts who write in the vernacular, the new dramatists have been much involved in the stage realization of their own plays, whether as producers, or as actors, or even both. The result has been to tilt the balance in favour of performance rather than publication. Many dramatists whose plays are yet to appear in print have featured prominently on university campuses and during state and national festivals of the arts. For some others, their published plays represent only a small part of their total output.

This kind of approach to drama is desirable because it emphasizes the fact that any dramatist's esteem has to begin with his audience and not his publishers. The bane of most early Nigerian drama in English has been its failure to appeal to more than a very small number of people, even among the so-called educated who constitute its potential audience. Most observers tend to blame this failure on a number of factors – the low level of literacy in the country, the lack of professional acting companies and the absence of regular theatre houses. But these are only half-truths, and they ignore a fundamental inadequacy of some of the plays themselves. Forms and techniques derived from classical Greek, Elizabethan or twentieth-century *avant-garde* plays may have their virtues, but a dramatist who relies on them must accept the risk of communicating with only those few members of his audience who are familiar with such techniques. The only way that any drama can make an impact on its environment is by reflecting it in its subject, theme and technique.

Drama is a social form, and a play that purports to be written for and about a people must inevitably rely on conventions that obtain for such

people. Drama, Esslin says, 'deals with the basic human emotions and
predicaments in a social context, both in the interaction of several
characters on the stage, and in the even more important interaction
between the stage and the audience'.[1] The implication is that any dramatist has to feel a greater commitment to his primary rather than his
international audience.

It is in this connection that Ola Rotimi is important as a leading
exponent of the crusade to remedy the lack of communication between
drama in English and the Nigerian audience. Four of his plays have been
published to date,[2] and each of them had proved a stage success before
appearing in print. Also, play-writing is only one aspect of Rotimi's
effort to make drama a process in which many can participate and find
satisfaction. In particular, he is to be remembered for founding the Ori
Olokun Theatre Company (now the University of Ife Theatre Company), a motley crew of university dons, students and self-employed or
unemployed artistes, both literate and illiterate, who performed his and
other dramatist's plays to audiences in many parts of the country.

Ola Rotimi makes no bones about writing primarily for a Nigerian
audience. Although he employs the English language, he consciously
attempts to reach out to Nigerians of different levels of proficiency in the
language:

> English . . . is the official medium of communication in Nigeria.
> Inevitably, I write for audiences who are knowledgeable in this lan-
> guage. However, in handling the English language in my plays, I
> strive to temper its phraseology to the ear of both the dominant
> semi-literate as well as the literate classes, ensuring that my dialogue
> reaches out to both groups with ease in assimilation and clarity in
> identification.[3]

In addition to such deliberately simplified language,

> . . . I try to anchor my play to a vivid story line. Nigerians like action.
> When we boil it down, really, the essence of drama is ACTION which,
> by Aristotelian definition, means plot, which in turn presumes a story
> line.[4]

At the initial stage, Rotimi's experiment did not seem to have been
viewed with much sympathy, especially by critics. The literary-minded
ones found his language rather offensive, and not many people cared to
consider such English as a conscious experiment. The following excerpt
from a review of *The Gods Are Not to Blame* is typical of the reaction to the
language of the play:

The blandness of the language aside, and the unsure oscillation between an unrecognizable Nigerian 'patoise' and great poetry and mag-
nificent language, there were descents to sheer bathos. There was an
abundance of banalities such as 'Talk your talk' and the absurd toying
with grand Yoruba saws produced in such phrases as 'Bad word' and
'Bad words with laughter', was, to say the least, embarrassing; the
inconsistencies manifested in the chafing-at-the-heels of such lines as
'Father consoles her' by *'Baba* takes the baby' made the audience
wince. And these are precisely the kinds of errors . . . which place *The
Gods Are Not to Blame*, at best, in the category of interesting apprentice work.[5]

Genuine banalities deserve criticism – and many of the instances cited by
the above critic are absent from the final, published version of the play, a
clear instance of the playwright's readiness to benefit from experience
gained in the light of audience reaction and criticism. But none of
Rotimi's critics showed exactly why such language was inappropriate.
For the actual weakness of the play is that language sounds a discordant
note in a play that attempts to arouse tragic feelings and emotions in its
audience. It is curious that a playwright who subscribes so much to
Aristotelian tenets, as is evident both from his adaptation of the quintes-
sence of Greek tragedy, *Oedipus Rex*, and part of his statement quoted
above, can ignore the Greek philosopher's insistence on elevated language as the appropriate register for the tragic genre.

In his preoccupation with reaching a wide audience, Rotimi sometimes resorts to literal translations of stock Yoruba expressions or poetic
types that draw attention to their incongruity rather than their profundity. Alongside instances of great poetry like the following,

> Crossing seven waters
> I, a son of the tribe of
> Ijekun Yemoja,
> found my way,
> to this strange land
> of Kutuje. I came
> to see suffering,
> and I felt suffering.
> 'Get up,
> Get up,' I said
> to them; 'not to do something
> is to be crippled fast. Up, up,
> all of you;
> to lie down resigned to fate
> is madness.
> Up, up, struggle: the world is
> struggle',[6]

can be found lapses like, 'If you need help, search for it first among
yourselves. Do not open your noses at me, I cannot help' (p. 13), which

come at serious moments in the play. Sometimes, too, Rotimi's diffuse style waters down Yoruba proverbs and witticism:

> All lizards lie prostrate: how can a man tell which lizard suffers from bellyache? In time, the pain will make one of them lie flat on its back, then shall that which has been unknown be made known. (p. 23)

But language is only one trait of the play that reveals an apprentice piece. The Oedipus myth provides Rotimi with the 'vivid story line' he desires, but how successfully has he transplanted this material in Nigerian soil? What is the motivation for the adaptation, and how well does the play succeed in this regard? Rotimi has pointed out that the title of the play presupposes a political thesis that warns the developing African nations not to put the blame for their shortcomings on their former colonial masters:

> '*The Gods Are Not to Blame*, does not refer to the mythological gods or mystic deities of the African pantheon. Rather it alludes to national, political powers such as America, Russia, France, England, etc. – countries that dictate the pace of world politics. The title implies that these political 'gods' shouldn't be blamed or held responsible for our own national fallings.[7]

He specifically intends this to apply to the Nigerian Civil War which had tribal distrust as one of its major causes. Odewale in the play is a man who is roused by his sense of patriotism, as well as his irascibility, to commit an act that later leads to his undoing.

The adaptation does not work well along this line, and part of the problem stems from Rotimi's imposition of the Greek world view on the Yoruba one. It is easy to draw, as he has done, superficial parallels between both cultures. There are Yoruba gods and goddesses that have their different offices, like the Greek deities, but their relationships with one another and with human beings differ fundamentally from the Greek ones. Instead of the awesome beings who pursue vengeance from generation to generation, and against whose judgement there is often no appeal, the Yoruba deities are benign beings who are willing to come to man's aid in times of trouble provided he is humble enough to call on them and follow their prescriptions. The very notion of fate is not the same in the two cultures. For the Greeks, it is something imposed by the gods; but for the Yoruba, fate is what each man chooses for himself prior to his entry into the living world, and it is uninfluenced by any other being, man or god. But even then, there is an escape route via the gods who are capable of mitigating the effect of any bad choice. Odewale means to explore this avenue when he takes his case to the oracle, but the voice he hears belongs to alien gods who grant no respite from human suffering:

VOICE:	You have a curse on you, son.
ODEWALE:	What kind of curse, Old one?
VOICE:	You cannot run away from it, the gods have willed that you will kill your father, and then marry your mother!
ODEWALE:	Me! Kill my own father, and marry my own mother?
VOICE:	It has been willed.
ODEWALE:	What must I do then not to carry out this will of the gods?
VOICE:	Nothing. To run away would be foolish. The snail may try, but it cannot cast off its shell. Just stay where you are . . . stay where you are . . .

(p. 60)

Staying where he believes to be his home would not have altered Odewale's fate, unless the gods are indeed the liars he presumptuously calls them. This is in fact one of the unconvincing statements that the playwright puts into his hero's mouth. Odewale never at any time attains a moment of awareness. He blames himself for his misfortunes but fails to understand that he could never have escaped the terrible fate that has been made his for no reason other than that the gods willed it. Sophocles' Oedipus comes to realize the futility of challenging the gods' will, and the chorus emphasizes man's subservience to the gods; but Odewale remains as blind as ever, and the judgement he pronounces on himself at the end of the play can only come from a confused mind. In the Greek context, the myth which the play explores at least makes Oedipus the sharer in a general inexorable curse that engulfs a whole house, but Odewale in *The Gods Are Not to Blame* suffers because the gods will it so. This over-riding sense of relentless fate destroys the political thesis that Rotimi wants the title of the play to imply.

More successful is Rotimi's reliance on non-linguistic techniques to communicate in the play. There is an extensive use of music, dance and sound effects to reinforce mood and meaning. Such elements can easily degenerate into sheer theatricality if they are only employed for orna-mental purposes, but Rotimi attempts to make them generate form and therefore reinforce the action of the play. He does not at this stage attain his best in this regard, but the Olurombi song at the beginning of Act Two, Scene 3, is a good example of how such elements can be made functional in a play. The scene looks homely enough: a mother has just told a story to her children, and she then leads them in singing the song. But the context of the song makes it clear that the playwright intends more than this depiction of a commonplace event. It comes from the story of a woman who swears to give anything as reward to the iroko spirit if she has a successful venture in the market. The request is granted, but she realizes her folly when the spirit demands her only child. Rotimi skilfully brings in the song to forebode disaster, especially as it comes after Odewale's fateful words, 'May my eyes not see Aderopo again till I die!' (p. 35).

Such a subtle use of song can communicate fully only with an audience that shares the playwright's cultural background. In the theatre, the outsider may partake of the mood of the rendition; but no reading, even if a translation is provided, can effect as rich a meaning as the playwright intends. This, however, does not amount to a defect as obscurity would not result even if the song were completely omitted. On the whole, then, *The Gods Are Not to Blame* is important not only for what it accomplishes but also for what it sets out to achieve. The search for a medium that can communicate with a wider audience has led the dramatist to explore techniques that give his plays a distinct Nigerian stamp.

Rotimi carries on this seach in his subsequent plays, *Kurunmi* and *Ovonramwen Nogbaisi*. The historical material he explores in each play provides him with the vivid story line that he desires, but in each case he has been careful to select and rearrange those aspects of the raw material that are relevant to his overall objective. Each play is a historical tragedy that concentrates on the fortunes of a central character in the general atmosphere of unrest and war.

In *Kurunmi* Rotimi achieves the twin objectives that he aims at in his first play. The career of Kurunmi (even as sketched in the historical note that accompanies the play) provides very suitable material for a tragic hero along the lines Rotimi subscribes to. Kurunmi is a man fighting a cause which he believes is just; he fails because he makes a fatal error of judgement but also because he is pitched against forces that he alone cannot withstand. Also, the historical background of a constitutional deadlock, unsuccessful peace moves and eventual war is easily recognizable as a parallel to the Nigerian Civil War, and so the socio-political objective he intends in his first play comes out more clearly here. Altogether, Rotimi has been careful not to divert attention from the main concern of the play. The series of battles that take place in Act Three are all important as aspects of the historical event, but the playwright's intention is not to recount the facts of history. Rather, he is interested in the study of man caught up in a particular situation. The battles are important because they help to focus attention on Kurunmi's changing fortunes before the final blow that spells his doom. Rotimi therefore avoids needless details. Each scene in which there is an encounter between the armies of Ijaiye and Ibadan carries the action of the play a step forward. Great economy is effected through the diary records of the Manns (Scenes 5 and 9), and the defeat of the combined army of Egba and Ijaiye marks the climax of the action and the downfall of Kurunmi.

Just as he has been careful in the selection of his material, Rotimi also pays greater attention to the appropriateness of language to the action which he depicts. There are still instances when the language provokes laughter, but these are moments calculated to effect comic interludes. Besides, such humour only serves to accentuate the tragic action, especially as most of the scorn comes ironically from Kurunmi himself and is directed at his enemies:

> The frog is kicked – Kpa!
> it flattens
> y-a-k-a-ta
> on its back.
> We shall all die
> 'gbere'
> We shall all die
> 'gbere'[8]

But quite apart from such instances Rotimi now takes greater pains to preserve the profundity of the traditional literary types he renders in English. Kurunmi's first speech is a good example of the poetic style that Rotimi tends towards in his translations of such materials:

The gaboon viper!
When the gaboon viper dies,
its children take up its habits,
poison and all.
The plantain dies,
its saplings take its place,
broad leaves and all.
The fire dies, its ashes
bear its memory with a shroud of white fluff . . .
Why, the pride of bees is in the honeycomb.
The pride of the weaver-bird
shows in the skilful design of its nest.
And where stands the pride of the monkey?
Is it not in his knowledge of the secrets on treetops?
The pride of man, my people,
is in his tradition –
something to learn from for the peace of his present:
something to learn from for the advance of his tomorrow. (pp. 15–16)

The language tends to be determined by the mood of the scene. There is an instance when Kurunmi's register changes completely as he drives a point home to the Reverend Mann:

KURUNMI: Reverend Mann, I don't think you ever had a
                father.
REV. MANN: Your Greatness!
KURUNMI: Oh, but it is true. If you had a father, Reverend
                Mann, the way you think would be different,
                very different from the way you think. Imagine
                me for a moment. I go to your country, and I tell
                your father: 'Mr So-and-So, from this day on, I
                want you to give up the ways of your fathers; cast
                away your manner of worship; neglect your ritu-
                als; Mr So-and-So, snub the shrines of your
                fathers; betray your gods.' Now Reverend Mann,
                how do you think your father would feel? (p. 35)

There is in the above examples no descent to the banal, no watering-down of thought for the benefit of a semi-literate audience. Rotimi has learnt to strike a balance between making concessions to the educational inadequacies of his audience and remaining true to his creative impulse.

In *Ovonramwen Nogbaisi*, Rotimi's language strikes a pitch that is deliberately poetic, judging from the diction and rhythm of a great deal of the lines. Graded language is one of the means by which each charac-ter's status is established. Oba Ovonramwen in particular is marked by his undeniably lofty language:

> Let the land know this: Ovonramwen Nogbaisi is henceforth set to rule as king after the manner of his fathers before him. Some men there are who think that, by honour of years, or the power of position, or by too much love for trouble, they can dull the fullness of my glow and bring darkness on the empire! They forget . . . They forget that no matter how long and stout the human neck, on top of it must sit a head. Henceforth, a full moon's my glow – dominant, and unopen to rivalry throughout the empire.[9]

The other chiefs and warlords are also, to a lesser extent, colourful in their language, but the white characters are marked by their plain, business-like manner of speech that aims at precision rather than embell-ishment. In contrast, the less important characters – the Edo citizens who serve the white man and the British officers' orderly – are made to speak ungrammatical and pidgin English.

The dramatic situation in *Ovonramwen* is not as compelling as in *Kurunmi*, but Rotimi makes up for this by employing music, song and chant to create a strong atmosphere of disaster throughout the play. Rotimi's technique here can hardly be surpassed in its brilliance.[10] The play relies heavily on elements from traditional Edo performances and more than ever, it becomes impossible to separate such elements from the development of the plot and the overall mood of the play. It is a classic example of an approach to drama which places greater emphasis on performance than on reading the play as literature. Yet there is nothing to suggest a reliance on theatrical elements just for their own sake. The translations of the songs and chants show that they are well integrated into the action of the play. The climax of Rotimi's technique is seen in the depiction of the battle between the Edo and the British armies, a masterpiece in art and economy:

> British martial music again; subliminal Benin war drums. Consul-General Moor appears, bearing the British flag flown from a medium-length pole. He advances towards Ologbosere who steps forward also – the two approaching centre-stage. Getting there, they both stop, some two yards apart. Low lights on Oba Ovonramwen watching the imminent confrontation.
>
> For a brief while, Ologbosere and Moor stand glaring at each other. Then, first slowly, the movement building up, they begin to stalk each other; feline malevolence. Suddenly, they attack – the stems of their national symbols strike together, and lock. Pressure is applied on both sides. For a while, a stalemate . . . then oscillation, as the one strains to weigh down the other. At last . . . gradually, painfully, Ologbosere begins to give ground – sinking lower and lower under the oppressive muscles of his opponent.
>
> British martial music swells forth, drowning the already dying beats of Benin war drums. Booms of cannon-fire from the British artillery, offstage. In that instant, Moor's soldiers – predominantly blacks led by British officers – pour on to stage from all directions with a deafening huzzah, wildly brandishing flaming torches. Ologbosere ducks and takes to his heels, Moor in hot pursuit, his soldiers following victoriously. (p. 43)

A dramatist who is always consciously experimenting in his plays is bound to come up with newer, better ideas that can make the dramatic experience richer for both artist and audience. But one thing is already evident from Rotimi's plays to date: he has found a technique that is adequate for the expression of the rich and complex cultural base from which his creative impulse develops. His experiment with the English language has shown that the choice of any language for communication implies that one's work is directed only to those who have attained at least an average degree of proficiency in that particular language. But in place of the deadlock that language presents, Rotimi finds that there are other elements worth exploring in a bid to make drama a process in which many more people can share and find delight. And there can be no better

proof of his success than the popularity his plays have gained within
Nigeria.

References
 1. Martin Esslin, 'Two Nigerian playwrights', in Ulli Beier (ed.), *Introduction to African Literature* (London, Longman, 1967), p. 255.
 2. The plays are, in order of publication:
    (i) *The Gods Are Not to Blame* (London, Oxford University Press, 1971).
    (ii) *Kurunmi* (London, Oxford University Press, 1971).
    (iii) *Ovonramwen Nogbaisi* (Benin City, Ethiope Publishing Corporation and Oxford University Press, 1974).
    (iv) *Our Husband Has Gone Mad Again* (Oxford University Press, 1977).
 3. B. Lindfors, *Dem-Say: Interview with Eight Nigerian Writers* (University of Texas, Austin, African and Afro-American Research Institute, 1974), p. 60.
 4. ibid. (Rotimi's emphasis.)
 5. Dapo Adelugba, 'Theatre critique', *Ibadan* (October 1969), p. 49.
 6. *The Gods Are Not to Blame*, p. 6. Further references will be inserted in the essay.
 7. Lindfors, op. cit., p. 61.
 8. *Kurunmi*, pp. 27–30. Further references will be inserted in the essay.
 9. *Ovonramwen Nogbaisi*, pp. 6–7. Further references will be inserted in the essay.
10. Rotimi admitted in an informal interview he granted this writer that he attains a level in his dramaturgy in the play that he himself finds so personally satisfactory that he is almost scared of attempting another play.

4

Ghanaian Poetry in the 1970s

▼▼▼▼▼▼▼▼▼▼▼▼▼▼▼▼▼▼▼▼▼▼▼▼▼▼▼▼▼▼

JAWA APRONTI

THE poetry scene in Ghana today presents an intriguing mosaic – a few well-known poets publishing new works, some of them fresh and delightful to read, others so stiff and incoherent as to constitute a disservice to writer and publisher alike. On the other hand, new voices are emerging, young (and some not so young) poets whose distinctive perceptions, turns of phrase, visions of society all augur well for the future of Ghanaian letters.

The most important development that these new poets have introduced into Ghanaian society in the 1970s has been the institutionalization of the poetry recital as a popular theatrical event, an occasion that attracts people from all walks of life. The recital has reinstated poetry as a public event in the African tradition, providing a point of confrontation between poet and audience, and thereby underlining the specifically public concerns of Ghanaian poetry. This confrontation, on stage as well as through radio and television, short-circuits the problems faced by all writers in Ghana, especially the young and aspiring ones – the frustrating delays encountered in the local publishing houses, which rob new works of whatever immediate frame of reference or freshness of address they may have had. Some manuscripts do get published by the state-owned Ghana Publishing Corporation, the largest publishing house in the country. But the selections done by the editors of the Corporation do not always represent the best judgements. There are many more exciting manuscripts which are gathering dust in various places, whilst recent titles announced by local publishing houses do not invest Ghanaian poetry of the 1970s with its true stature. The hallmark of this poetry remains the emergence of individual volumes by an increasing number of poets. Considering the constraints on publication, constraints which often border on virtual strangulation, this is a noteworthy achievement. It is to these two categories of emerging poetry, the published as well as the unpublished, that this essay addresses itself. The aim of this study is to isolate the major trends in this corpus, to relate them to the situation of individual poets and to offer some projections about the future course of Ghanaian poetry.

During the period under review, three established poets who have spent varying periods abroad have published individual volumes of poetry and, incidentally, have now settled at home. They are Albert Kayper-Mensah, Kofi Awoonor and Joe de Graft. Kayper-Mensah spent several years in the Foreign Service. His *Dark Wanderer*[1] encapsulates his bifocal cultural experience, the African and the European. He is a prolific poet, having turned out two large and two small volumes within the decade, and is awaiting the publication of several more volumes, some of which are quite experimental in conception and execution.

Kayper-Mensah combines quantity of output with an uneven quality of expression. Whereas *Sankofa*[2] is an ingenious and original attempt to explore the poetic range of the epigrammatic symbols embossed on adinkra (originally funeral) cloth, Kayper-Mensah's other volume, *Akwaaba*,[3] represents a very indifferent level of attainment. Indeed the smaller volume *Sankofa* adumbrates some of the infelicities and irritating obscurities of the larger volume. Contrast, for instance, the expressiveness and unpretentiousness of

> Fertility is an okro fruit
> With a thousand seeds
> But hides them all in a dull exterior
> Till mature and dry for sowing

with the ungainly gait and clumsy final two lines of another adinkra poem on the same page:

> When our twins came
> Our four hearts linked;
> Found a centre in our name.
> Our shared hopes flowed
> Through it freely till we felt the same. (p. 36)

The poet's exploration of the lyrical potential of these graphic adinkra symbols is commendable but largely unsuccessful. Opportunities to make memorable verse of these familiar symbols are lost in cryptic, unrhythmic formulations. One savours with delight a haiku-like terseness in an adinkra poem, only to have one's pleasure cut short by the jerky line structure or cadence of the next one. *Sankofa*, in short, represents a middling effort.

Akwaaba is even less successful. The poet's turn of phrase is distinctly obsolescent. Two examples will suffice to prove the point:

> Not if we adorn
> The Christian's grave
> Serve we best his memory. (p. 24)

> The spider's fragile web
> Is firm enough to keep its
> Trapped fly kept, to die . . . (p. 47)

Such flaws abound in Kayper-Mensah's work, revealing in the poet an insensitive ear to the type of cadence that makes the most pleasing poetry. Many of the poems refuse to yield any meaning, however closely one tries to read them. An example is this excerpt from 'The Virgin and the Fanatic':

> Doubt? A meaningless
> Impediment, not here met
> Yet, in politics or faith. (p. 21)

In much of Kayper-Mensah the art is so obscurely formulated that it lies buried under the weight of words chosen without enough attention to their usual signification in the English language. Furthermore, all this exists side by side with glimpses of the aesthete trying to break out into song, as this excerpt from 'Tour Ghana: Know Ghana' reveals:

> Some there should be, who should bathe
> Our landscape in a fairer light
> Of intellect and passion
> To help the stranger see and think on
> **What her finer stranger see and mused on**
> Well beyond the ordinary . . . (p. 13)

The title poem in *The Drummer in Our Time*[4] has a harmonious blend of theme and style, a projection in this particular poem into the technological age but all cast in lilting rhythm and unlaboured diction. The poem flows with an effortless fluidity, a tenor that befits its idealistic and patriotic tone. Indeed, it is such an apocalyptic vision that tends to bring out the best in Kayper-Mensah, especially when this preoccupation is conjoined with that of the aesthete. 'Four Hours a Day' (pp. 64-7) is in this vein, in which the poet urges the reader to devote this fraction of the day to pursuits that ennoble the spirit:

> . . . four hours a day
> Spent in pleasures free from money making
> That a meditative Amo [*sic*] on odurja
> Hand in hand with a Bach may spread a mood

Of deepening contemplation on our thoughts,
Lead them through a world of revealing mirrors,
Hold in check stampeding, warring passions,
Chain them to some strong silk-cotton tree
Of an aesthetic principle that guides
Our energies into acts meaning love . . .

The second established poet is Kofi Awoonor, now teaching English at the University of Cape Coast. In *Rediscovery* (1964) he had made his mark as a poet heavily influenced by the tradition of oral poetry. Indeed, in *Keepers of the Sacred Wood* (1974) he paid glowing tributes to the work of three Ewe-medium poet-cantors who were instrumental in carrying forward the tradition into which he was born. In both *Night of My Blood*[5] and *Ride Me, Memory*[6] he extends the range of this borrowed voice, and largely expunges those somewhat unconventional tricks of syntax by which he sought in 1964 to evoke an aura of Ewe speech rhythms. *Ride Me, Memory* is in two parts, 'American Profiles' and 'African Memories'. It is very much a work executed away from home, at a distance that enables the poet to indulge at times in detached self-mockery. The section 'Long Island Sketches' contains several examples of this mature, controlled style, as this excerpt indicates:

The proclamation came first
in pencil. You must address me doctor
Puzzled beyond words I send polite inquiries
doctor of what? Of letters, words,
oral examinations, course works,
brilliant essays on Hopkins and Eliot . . .

If the above does not sufficiently indicate Awoonor's debt to Ewe poetry, the next section, entitled 'Songs of Abuse', forcefully highlights the poet's experiment in transmuting experience. Poetry of abuse, as Awoonor depicts it in *Keepers of the Sacred Wood*, is an important aspect of Ewe traditional poetry. It is very earthy, as this excerpt from 'To my Uncle Jonathan' indicates:

You fucker of sheep and goats
a pederast in bloomers
a whiskered fool with an obscene mouth.

Poems of abuse are intermittently teasing, jocular and bawdy. The tone of the second section, 'African Memories', is mellower. Indeed, the final poem, 'To Those Gone Ahead', is a sombre recall of memories of dead relatives, the imagery redolent with the exiled poet's nostalgia for home. If the grandmother is a gazelle, the grandfather is a hippo:

> And I, Awoonor, the dropsied
> seed from ancient loins
> wander here where there is winter
> birdsong and a yellow moon.

Night of My Blood is *Rediscovery* writ large; two-thirds of the earlier collection reappear in the latter, some of them slightly revised. The best among the poems in the earlier volume do still retain their freshness, giving proof of the poet's success in integrating himself within his indigenous tradition and therefore being able to project, as he does in his invocation to his muse in 'My God of Song was Ill' (*Night*, p. 22), an image of a prodigal son whose psyche seems almost never to have left home. But even here some of the imagery can jar on the ear, as in 'So I walked in with my backside', where translation from the Ewe might have been rendered a little more idiomatically in order to bring the line into tune with the serious tone of the poem.

The new poems in *Night of My Blood* provide much evidence that Awoonor has expanded his range of expression without sacrificing those insights that emanate from his fidelity to the tradition of oral poetry that launched him in the first place. This is still poetry of the speaking voice, of the narrator cognizant of the presence of his audience. Nature is as alive in this new poetry as it was in the earlier pieces. 'Lament of the Silent Sister', a poem dedicated to Chris Okigbo, is in this vein. It succeeds by the strength of its extended images that blend the swell of the floods with the procreative act and interpret the recall of Okigbo's memory through this medium; and the recurrent flood melts into the other elements, as they together attend with the poet the re-emergence of the presence of the hero of the poem.

Even in these new works, Awoonor's preoccupation with death is evident. This is a theme which provides the occasion for the injection of lamentations interlarded with echoes of the hymnal and the liturgy. Such lines conjoin the worlds of the living and the dead. 'Hymn To My Dumb Earth' (*Night*, pp. 82–95) is an ambitious poem conceived after this fashion but, in both title and content (witness the refrain, 'Everything comes from God'), the poet's attitude to religion remains ambiguous, despite a host of similes derived from Christianity. The final impression of Awoonor is of a predominantly sad poet, hooked almost on the elegiac, calling from the brink of the underworld to the living community.

The third established poet who is now back at home is Joe de Graft, well known as playwright, director and actor, and now teaching drama at the University of Ghana. *Beneath the Jazz and Brass*,[7] his first collection of verse, shows his grounding in indigenous tradition, despite a tendency to derive his imagery, and therefore his verse, from a fairly remote era of British poetry. *Jazz and Brass* gives ample evidence that de Graft is a careful craftsman. The dates he helpfully appends to the poems reveal that several of them have undergone revision, sometimes over a period of as long as twenty-one years. The collection shows a variety of themes, moods and styles. There are some quintessentially poetic moments, as in 'Dirge to My Father', notably in the refrain:

> Yet hug him gently to your breast
> Good earth, Mother of us all
> Hug him gently
> For from his loins I sprang. (p. 96)

The poet's constant preoccupation, however, is with public themes. In 'Mothers, Give Us Pause from the Frenzy', de Graft censures the contemporary society for carelessly watching its patrimony decay, for not bringing its creativity to bear on the tasks of the day. He prays:

> And, O Mother Africa
> When the drums sound again
> May they be drums
> New-sculptured by *these* hands, not our fathers'
> Membraned with the skin of elephants
> *We ourselves* have haunted . . . (p. 36)

A similar call to his generation is underscored in 'City on an Anthill' where Accra emerges as a 'prince of squalid cities'. The poet moves effortlessly from themes such as these to expressions of solidarity with the beggar and the stone-breaker, the downtrodden of an unjust society, to some delicately wrought love poems. The following excerpt reveals a sureness of touch and a felicity of expression:

> They say that out of heavenly harmony
> God the maker framed this universe;
> But from the ashes of this nightmare waste
> Shall rise another world,
> Quickened by the light from your eyes
> And the tender warmth of your smile. (p. 15)

The logic of many love poems demands that superhuman attributes should be ascribed to the loved one. De Graft executes this in a spectacular finale in the closing lines of 'Resurrection'.

Allegiance to his indigenous tradition is couched in de Graft's poetry in terms other than those usually associated with Awoonor. Where Awoonor borrows the formal voice of that tradition, de Graft seizes on the substance of his patrimony; where Awoonor transmutes the very language of the traditional poem, making it echo into English via the poet as medium, de Graft projects the claims of that tradition in learned, almost bookish, imagery. This is an excerpt from 'African Studies':

> This picking of poor men's brains to sell as one's own for the highest
>   bid on the American Grants market,
> And this desecration of holy shrines,
>   eaves-dropping on the conversations of gods;
> This predacity,
>   This hogging of every new talent that shows its golden face above the
>   soil of Africa,
> Or this heady exaltation of every hunk of turd dropped by an African
>   cow . . . (p. 38)

In spite of the strong feeling, the tone and texture of the verse have a literary flavour. De Graft's reading shows through his poetry. But this is not to deny his rich variety of moods, themes and styles.

If we accuse Awoonor of a tendency towards a morbid outlook on life, with E. Y. Egblewogbe we enter a region of unrelieved gloom. His *Wizard's Pride*⁸ brings together poems previously published in a literary journal and some hitherto unpublished works. In the introduction, Egblewogbe affirms that 'the apparent humorous tone [of "Too Late"] is to be found in all the piece, that have love as their theme'. But this expression of intention is hardly realized. In fact, *The Wizard's Pride* is a catalogue of almost unrelieved gloom. The following lines from an apparent love poem are typical:

> Come, stay for once and we shall prove
> That this celestial bliss
> Is meant for you and me; for us to taste
> Before wrinkled time comes feeling for
> Our faces; before chilly death
> Drags our decaying bodies into muddy graves. (p. 28)

It is difficult to see the 'apparent humorous tone' in this supposedly joyous love poem. After a brief interlude of brightness the poet quickly relapses into the grip of death:

> That when ash to ash is gone, our holy angel,
> Cupid, should lead us
> To Eternity
> Of
> Love. (p. 28)

Not even the importation of Cupid from across the seas can relieve the gloom. Egblewogbe does not permit joy to come to fruition; hardly does

happiness blossom forth than the poet bludgeons it into the grave.
Occasionally, he manages to sing of happiness by invoking strikingly
surprising images, as in this brief poem titled 'Beauty':

> I once loved a beauty and
> Great happiness was mine.
> But now the wheel has turned,
> And, what thoughts at the sight of one!
> The fly on a thorn tree;
> Deceit behind a handsome face;
> The mosquito on a dead man's toe. (p. 26)

Aside from an obsolescence of tone, the images in the concluding two
lines are sinister and morbid. And the man in the final line is, as one
might expect, dead.

Egblewogbe combines this morbid outlook with a diction of yes-
teryear and syntactical patterns equally out of date. His poetry is full of
expressions such as: .

> To swell the Angelic numbers (p. 8)
> Dipt in Songs celestial, I should (p. 10)
> Still I am minded to travel on (p. 16)
> Oh, you may sojourn there awhile (p. 27)
> The students slumbered free (p. 34)

With his range of vision so severely restricted, his syntax and diction
derived from an unresurrectible era of the English language, and his
lack of inspiration from local lore or practice, Egblewogbe appears to be
heading for a dead end.

Kwakuvi Azasu presents in his *Streams of Thought*[9] a more exciting
poetic visage and voice, displays a keener eye for the dramatic and
explores a wider range of themes. For example, 'The Nightmare of the
Labourer' shows an agility of mind, even though superficially the
theme is reminiscent of Egblewogbe:

> Dreamily I grope on; clawing at the air
> To grab bare bones of my kind
> Scrapped clean of Flesh and marrow!
> Dazed, I plod on the dark wilderness of the world
> Treading on pieces of decaying flesh at places
> And kicking dry bones at some;
> At some I hear the sucking at bone for marrow
> And some the noisy munching of meat and whispers.
> Staggering steadily on, I arrive at a stranger spot . . .

The persona pursues his experiences, but rises above the decay and
images of death. He affirms life, even attains a semblance of nobility:

> Coming to, I lay a surprised hold
> on my matchet and worn out hoe
> And realize the sun is sinking now
> But I must scrap the soil . . .
> With all the horrors I have just seen
> How can I blame any,
> For not being taller than calumny.

Streams of Thought contains errors which a more careful editing might have removed before the publication of the modest volume. But it is the work of an unmistakably inventive and resourceful poet – a poet moreover of *action*, and therefore life-radiating. This dramatic description of Huhunya Falls (pp. 58–9)

> . . . a twirling
> and churning
> a tearful confusion
> and splashing
> and gurgling suffocation
> and spouting
> and twisting
> in the roar and spray and foam
> and pouring
> and splattering
> and whirling . . .

is the more delightful when one recalls the laziness of pace evoked in the opening lines:

> Leisurely it meanders
> on, on and on
> and along it unfurls
> and roves the wide, wide valley,
> the open galley on the plateau . . .

It is true that 'leisurely' does not sit too well in the opening line, but the point is that Azasu has demonstrated an accomplished artist's discernment of how to dictate and simulate pace. There are enough signs of future development in this energetic young man to make us look forward to his next volume.

Lawerh Therson-Cofie has yet to publish an independent volume, but his appearances in anthologies and at poetry recitals over the past eight years indicate the emergence of a powerful voice among Ghanaian poets of the younger generation. A journalist, he is best remembered for his 'Zimbabwe and Namibia Prelude'[10] a poem written nearly ten years ago in which the poet asserts the determination of the oppressed black majority of southern Africa to take control of their destiny. By employing the techniques of parallel structures and a redolent refrain,

Therson-Cofie makes a forceful statement in the cause of liberation:

> We
> Sons of Opanin Bibini
> Who cover our faces with black calico
> We shall take our bows and arrows
> We shall brandish our spears.
> Those tiger skins besmeared with our fathers' blood
> Shall be our armour
> The great walls of Kilimanjaro
> The Drakensberg, the Cameroun
> The Kenya and the Atlas
> All shall be our shields
> And the waters of the Nile
> The Congo, the Niger, the Zambesi
> And the Volta shall heal our wounds.

The poet conscripts the African soil and her physical features into the liberation army; he invokes the spirits of fallen heroes, resurrects them and puts them at the vanguard of the liberation army. The poem is not unique among recent Ghanaian poems in its commitment to continental liberation. All such poems affirm with a resoluteness reminiscent of Nkrumah's Ghana the determination to link the liberation of the country with that of the whole continent.

The creative writing clubs established in secondary schools and training colleges across Ghana in the 1960s, and the new avenue provided by public readings and recitals of poetry have together contributed to the emergence of many new poetic voices in Ghana. One of the most notable is the winner of the first prize in the 1976 VALCO Literary Awards contest, Kofi Anyidoho. Like Kofi Awoonor, an Ewe, Anyidoho has absorbed much traditional Ewe poetry; but they both constitute extensions of that mode, for their individual stamp is discernible in their verse. In the case of Anyidoho, this is represented by a toughness of texture, an ability to explore variations of a single theme. The excerpt below, from the poem, 'Go Tell Jesus', from his unpublished collection, 'Brain Surgery', is typical of his nimbleness of intellect:

> Go
> Go ask Jesus
> Whether He really said
> We cannot reach our God
> If we do not pass through Him
> Tell Him to tell you
> The fate of my ancestors
> Who lived and died before
> He the Christ was born
> Will all of them be
> damned?

Anyidoho's is poetry of the speaking voice. More than Awoonor but
definitely less than Egblewogbe, he reveals a tendency to the elegiac. He
has titles such as 'A Dirge for Christmas' and 'A Dirge of Joy'. In the
latter the poet does make a call for a joyful song, but this call is stated in
a dirge:

> Young Clansman,
>   harvester of stunted yams and oyster shells,
>   return these elegies to your god of songs,
>   come back soon with tunes fit for the festival
>   of new hopes
> These dirges kill our little joys.

The theme of death and destruction is pervasive; the mood is predominantly gloomy, the tone sombre. But Anyidoho's treatment of
funereal themes does incorporate sometimes a critical detachment from
the subject, a hint almost of macabre humour and satire, as in this
specification of the surgeons that are to perform brain surgery on Nana
Africana, in the title poem of the collection:

> Bending over him
>   are the reverend figures of
>   three Master-Brain-Surgeons:
>   the first suffers from fits of forgetfulness,
>   the second they say, is a retired drunkard,
>   and the third a natural clown of the first
>   degree.

Naturally, the poet casts doubt on their diagnosis of 'chronic psy-
chedislocation' and 'morbid melancholia'.

Even in poems with foreign settings, Anyidoho shows little joy. Invariably we are given tragic forebodings, a sadly depleted patrimony, the
agony of a wanderer struggling to get back home, as in these words
addressed to Ralph Crowder in Alabama:

> You may come
> Crowder
> You may come
> But O! Brother!
> all is not well at home
> all is not well with us
> we shall welcome you back home
> we shall pour libation to our gods
> But there is little, very little to give you . . .

Anyidoho leaves an impression of moroseness, although he is not as
fatalistic as Egblewogbe. He lacks Awoonor's occasional explosions of
joy, even in his light-hearted excursions into abuse.

It seems appropriate to conclude this essay with the most picturesque Ghanaian poet of the 1970s, the man who turned the poetry recital into a popular public event: Atukwei Okai, friend of Voznesensky and Yevtushenko. In a review article[11] I traced Okai's development up to the publication of his *Oath of the Fontomfrom and other Poems* (1971). It will therefore be sufficient for the present purpose to deal solely with the only volume that has appeared since then, *Lorgorligi Logarithms*, and note that the next collection 'Rhododomdroms in Donkeydom' has been with his local publishers for a long time and should be available very soon.

As the titles of his collections confirm, Okai is a poet of sounds, a musical and rhythmical poet. One says this by way of isolating his predominant mood and tenor, not with a view to asserting these as his only qualities or indeed of denying such qualities to other poets. His earlier work shows a tendency to indulge this love of sound a little too much in places. Whereas Okai has largely overcome his earlier penchant for alliteration, or rather tamed that predilection and subjected it to the overall demands of specific poems, one still notices a reluctance to use direct expressions, a pursuit of bombastic effect in contexts where this does not exactly contribute to the elucidation of meaning.

The oracular quality of Okai's poetry has been noted by commentators. He combines direct invocation of famous, and sometimes comparatively obscure, personages with a playing on the sounds of words that chime in his mind, thus managing to drive home a point many times over. Here is his description of the enthusiasm with which students (and incidentally the general population) embraced the task of nation-building in the wake of the January 1972 coup:

for with the sugarcane cutlasses
of asutsuare and komenda
your brothers and sisters
the ghano-africans

are cutting down and burning down
the heavy gaudy gowns of their minds
gowns that have been blinds
in their minds

blinds in their minds
soul-ensickening blinds in their minds
cobweb-encased blinds in their minds
soot-spawning blinds in their minds
gangrene-growing blinds in their minds
blinding blindman blinds in their minds.

In my earlier essay on Okai's growth, I called attention to the torrential swell of his verse. The inattentive reader, not taking Okai for a riddler and a speaker in parables, will fail to catch the sense of his poetry. In his long pieces these come in cycles that are interlarded with seeming digressions. But they only seem to digress. They are the links that bind the nodes of thought into chains of meaning. After all *Lorgorligi* in his mother tongue denotes deviousness, indirection, riddling. And in the title poem that incorporates *lorgorligi*, the nodes of thought point to a disappointment with the course of national affairs; the personae addressed (as opposed to the great ones that are invoked) are mostly the writers, the peasants, the dispossessed of the land.

> woman! woman!
> how often you carry the heaviness
> of your soul . . . only to empty it into songs . . .
>
> though our dialectic has been arrested
> and frozen in mid-season
> yet the algebra of the revolution
> is being worked out . . . (p. 51)

The closing lines situate the poet's faith in the future, thus making Okai not a merely sad or tragic poet, but one with a sense of direction, whose cries of agony are backed by analysis of the 'dialectic' (his own word!) underlying the course of human history. This is what animates his elegy to Nkrumah, titled 'Chain Gang – Soul Autopsy' (pp. 63–81), a poem enriched by the heroic chants of the African peoples in consonance with the continental significance of the dead hero. Okai's invocation of the funeral is replete with the dedication of those who *know* the meaning of Nkrumah's life:

> all africa is coming to see you off
> all the people are coming to bear you home
> the throat-tightening tears of the toiling
> tenants of the earth choke the soul
>
> who was not present at your creation
> am now present at your cremation
> not your father nor your mother
> is the chief mourner – all
> the common people of Africa are
>
> all the way from cairo through aswan . . .

Okai's poetry, despite the occasional deviousness of the riddler and speaker of parables, is often direct and explicit, pulling together from the

rich store of his reading and his experience associative ideas that embell-
ish his thought and give it substance.

Ghanaian poetry in the 1970s faces problems of publication, which
have prevented some very distinctive new voices from emerging. For
example, the works of Kodjo Laing and Kobena Acquah are as exciting
as Anyidoho's; they all have collections awaiting the attention of any
sympathetic publisher. Meanwhile, the stage and the media offer them
access to the local audience. Some projections have been hazarded about
the likely paths of development of some of the poets whose works have
been looked at. The extent to which their poetry will continue to be
relevant to the concerns of their society will depend on the extent to
which they, in their turn, are willing to serve as spokesmen of that society
– proclaimers of its woes, exalters of its victories, bards of its hopes.

References
1. *The Dark Wanderer* (Tubingen, Horst Erdmann Verlag, 1970).
2. *Sankofa, Adinkra Poems* (Tema, Ghana Publishing Corporation, 1976).
3. *Akwaaba* (Tema, Ghana Publishing Corporation, 1976).
4. *The Drummer in Our Time* (London, Heinemann, 1975).
5. Kofi Awoonor, *Night of My Blood* (New York, Doubleday, 1971).
6. *Ride Me, Memory* (New York, Greenfield Review Press, 1973).
7. Joe de Graft, *Beneath the Jazz and Brass* (London, Heinemann, 1975).
8. *The Wizard's Pride and Other Poems* (Tema, Ghana Publishing Corporation, 1974).
9. *Streams of Thought* (Accra, Mpaba Educational Publications, 1974).
10. 'Zimbabwe and Namibia Prelude', *Okyeame*, 5 (1972), pp. 13–15.
11. Jawa Apronit,'John Atukwei Okai – the growth of a poet', *Universitas*, II, 1 (October 1972).

5
Atukwei Okai
and his Poetic Territory

▼▼▼▼▼▼▼▼▼▼▼▼▼▼▼▼▼▼▼▼▼▼▼▼▼▼▼▼▼▼

KOFI ANYIDOHO

> I, Oshamraku Atukwei, standing
>   before your shrine declare
>   myself by appointment the
>   organ-grinder to God and Man.
> Reality is responsible for my subconscious . . .
> your songs are responsible for my
> inner tensions . . . my dreams
> are in pain . . . though you hear no
> screams.[1]

IN these words Atukwei Okai announces his arrival upon the poetic scene in Africa. He seems to be in no doubt about his qualifications and the nature of his calling. He is ordained by the creator-god. He is not just a poet but a poet-cantor with a priest-like function. His songs may start from his subconscious but their burden is founded on reality, and it is a disturbing reality which fills his soul with inner tensions. Part of the reality, he suggests elsewhere, consists in a breakdown in communication between God and man:

> The switch-board in God's chamber is jammed!
> Walls. Walls. Please, be still . . .
>
> (*Oath*, p. 74)

But the poet does not seek to blame his people's loss of social balance on any negligence on the part of God. As a poet-cantor, he sees in himself a source of inspiration for his fallen race to rise again to reach out for their pride and their god:

> My brothers,
>   my people,

```
                              my brothers:
Fontomfrom! . . . . . . . . Fontomfrom!
I am
        the Fontomfrom –
                              listen!
Of you the living,
I am
        the Fontomfrom –
                              listen
Fontomfrom! . . . . . . . . Fontomfrom!
```
                                                    (*Oath*, pp. 20–1)

In 'Prelude', Okai, poet, organ-grinder, and Fontomfrom, anticipates the reactions of some of his own brothers to his song and his authority:

```
You ask:
Which is
My territory
I reply
This is my song. You ask: By whose authority,
I reply
Who says
I am wrong
```
                                                    (*Oath*, pp. 70–1)

This reply raises two central questions about Okai's poetry in particular, and African poetry in general. What is the validity of this type of poetry? By what criteria must it be judged? These questions have been thoroughly discussed in the general context of African literature and it might seem tedious to take them up again. But they are particularly relevant to Okai's poetry and an essay on him might well start with a brief look at these same questions.

Atukwie Okai is an important poet in the recent history of the development of African literature. His importance derives mainly from the nature and scope of the linguistic experimentation that goes on in his poems. Most African critics as well as some writers have declared that the African writer's task is complicated by the fact that he must use a borrowed language to record experiences which are mostly native to his own culture. Okai does not seem to be troubled by any such supposed complication. Rather, he defiantly flings his poetry in the general direction of his audience, as if to say, 'See, the white man's language is not my burden, I can handle it well enough and in my own way.' He is not the first or only African writer engaged in this type of thing, but he is certainly the boldest in the scope of his experimentation. This is not to say that he is automatically the greatest poet in Africa today. One could be important in any field of human endeavour without necessarily being great. Okai is important for the daring nature of his linguistic experimentation. The question of his greatness is another thing, to be settled with reference to the extent of his success with the experiment. This question will be taken up in the rest of this essay.

Reaction to Okai's poetry has been varied and contradictory. Some greet him with cheers and generous praise such as appear in the blurb of *Lorgorligi Logarithms*:

> the 'enfant terrible' of the Ghana Cultural scene; the new Guy Warren of Ghana who can put the old wine into new bottles; one of the foremost African poets; a first-rate craftsman whose poetry of arresting, startling imagery is the music of Africa; the Picasso of modern African poetry.

Others, however, have little difficulty in dismissing Okai's poetry as 'mere verbiage'. A particularly disparaging assessment of Okai's standing as a poet comes from K. K. Dei-Annang in his review of *Oath of the Fontomfrom and Other Poems*. The following concluding paragraph sums up Dei-Annang's reactions to Okai's verse:

> . . . unlike his non-African contemporaries, John Okai's path is beset with the insidiously fatal trap in the fact that, as an African poet, he may wish to write 'African' poetry. Whether there is any legitimately distinguishable form of the art which is entitled to such a name is not a matter that can be adequately discussed here. What is important is the embarrassing fact that the recent history of writing in Africa is littered with literary skeletons of countless would-be writers whose unrecognized (and therefore unchecked) hubris led them from writing poems *in* Africa into the fatal wish to write '*African*' poetry.[2]

Thus Dei-Annang dismisses Okai for the very reason that others admire him: that his poetry is distinctively *African*. Dei-Annang quotes a portion of Okai's 'Prelude', and declares: 'Well, this, at least, is *not* English poetry, nor even poetry in English.' But it is a strange somersault in logical reasoning to move from this statement to a position that denies the existence of such a thing as 'African' poetry. Dei-Annang falls victim to the prescriptions of what he calls 'serious students of literary aesthetics' or 'contemporary connoisseurs'. In Africa the poetic art still exists in oral form, and poetry has not as yet 'liberated itself from both the drum and the dance'. Okai's poetry clearly and boldly seeks to establish a link between written and oral poetry and it is not very helpful trying to evaluate it strictly 'on the chaste witness of the printed page'. It calls for a readjustment of critical approach, of the kind suggested by the Nigerian critic, Abiola Irele:

. . . the very differentiation that marks the two frames of reference of this literature imposes upon the critical function important adjustments of those principles worked out in the Western tradition, to the peculiar modes of sensibility which feature in the African works, and which derive from the African background, of which the uses of language, both conditioned by and conditioning the traditional modes of feeling and apprehension, constitute a distinct social reality.[3]

The foregoing remarks are not meant to be an apology for what might be genuine flaws in Okai's craftsmanship. The very nature of his approach to poetry carries with it a fundamental burden. There is the constant need to reconcile the peculiar nuances of two distinct linguistic media, each with its own artistic traditions. This is a troublesome burden for any poet and Okai may not always handle it with success. For example, the 'Fifth Ofruntum, Gong-Four: Chain Gang – Soul Autopsy' of the long poem 'Tinkongkong! Ayawaso' (*Lorgorligi*, pp. 63–81) is a strange song, a curious experiment in linguistic stylistics. It is meant to be a lament on the death of Kwame Nkrumah, but it is a very unusual lament. On the surface, it is a jumble of familiar tunes and echoes from diverse linguistic-cultural backgrounds. There is the Christian preacher's voice linked to the nostalgia of Negro spirituals and to political catch-phrases from the lips of street-boys; in the background we hear a chorus of Akan voices invoking ancestral gods. They sing to the rhythm of the talking drums, and at intervals the mournful tone of the hornblowers' dirge is captured in appropriate poetic expression. There are also voices in Hausa and Ga trying to comfort us by saying 'Baalefi' (It's all right) and 'Efee noko' (It doesn't matter). Other voices in Ga and Nzema bid us farewell while we receive greetings in Mampruli from folks at home saying 'Pusiyini'.

In this poem we see most clearly the eclectic nature of Okai's art. There are no linguistic boundaries to his poetic territory. We see also what difficulties such a method may run into if not handled with craft: a jumble of voices (and sounds) each striving too loud to be heard above the others. If carried to the extreme, its effect could be bewildering. Only with much homework and cross-references could some of the details be made to fall into place in the overall sense-scheme. Perhaps the poet does not need not put his readers and hearers to all that trouble, and there is also the danger that the poem may lose its artistic and imaginative balance and crumble into a confused heap. In the end what saves this poem from total chaos is the underlying unity of theme and mood. The real failure in this poem, however, is not that the reader-hearer is bewildered by a babble of tongues, but that, too often, the essential poetic voice flags, losing the pith appropriate to the mood of the lament.

The poet gives way to the radio announcer or town-crier or even to the master-of-ceremonies at a mad political rally. There is also a little too much of the

> lead kindly light
> lead kindly light
> AMID THE ENCIRCLING GLOOM.

This makes portions of the poem drag with the tediousness of an over-used processional hymn. But the poem is not a total failure. If it is weak and trite in portions, it is redeemed by moments of artistic excellence, like the lines on the *mmenson*, in which we find balance and beauty in the coalescence of sound and sense:

> the seven horns of the solemn *mmenson*
> mourn and moan their dirge upon the dead
> the memories of the *mmenson* haunt the dawn
> the memories of the *mmenson* haunt the morn
>
> (*Lorgorligi*, p. 69)

While this poem provides evidence of some of the worst dangers of Okai's poetic craft, it also points to some of the possibilities that exist for a poet with diverse linguistic-cultural resources to draw upon.

Most critics of Okai's poetry, admirers and detractors alike, are agreed on at least one point: that much of his poetry exhibits a certain imbalance in the adjustment of sound to sense. Okai himself once, at a public recital, reacted to this objection by declaring that it does not make sense to insist on separating the sound qualities of words from their meaning. But this is beside the point. The objection is not that his poetry is only sounds but rather that he sometimes gives much of it which does not create any sensible impression. As a poet consciously working out a link with the oral medium, he needs to make maximum use of sound effects. But surely there must be a limit to even this maximum, in spite of Nwoga's observation that in Okai's poetry sound is more important 'as a means to sense than the meaning of words'.[4] Too often Okai oversteps the boundaries of sound-sense and gets into the area of what sounds like noise. It is true that, as with Christopher Okigbo, we can enjoy Okai without fully grasping the logic of his verse, and any attempts to work out a consistent logic for it may only destroy our spontaneous joy. Unfortunately, however, he does not always exhibit the necessary control which we find Okigbo exercising over his words, their sounds and the images they suggest. It is not always easy, if at all possible, to identify any meaningful connection between the sounds of his words, and though we may be 'impressed' by the clever conjunction of sounds, even our sensory or emotional experience remains unordered. Where images are suggested by the sounds and/or 'intrinsic structure' of the words, such images remain blurred.

There is more to Okai's poetry than just sound and a conscious attempt to establish a link with the oral tradition. There are other explanations for the attraction and fascination of his songs. Some of these are his preoccupation with social problems, his imagery, sense of humour and dramatic presentation of ideas and events, as well as the energy which constitutes an undercurrent of his verse.

Okai has been described by some as a love poet. There is much truth in this. Among his works are such easily identifiable love poems as 'Flower-fall', 'Jonice', 'Pastoral Prelude', 'Nocturnal Prelude', 'Rosimaya', 'Fugue for Fireflies' and 'Dreamdom Communique to Valerieville'. Most of these are in part praise songs to the beauty and perfection of a lover, but they are also explorations of the poet's own emotional state as conditioned by the lover's qualities. The turbulence of his passions is often captured in appropriate imagery and verse movement:

```
gigantic and gentle in our homing joy
we journey
              towards
                    the centre
                          of our
tenderness . . .
and the prairie fires in my skin all hail thee
and the honey hunters
                    in my lips
                          all hail thee
and the night antelopes
                    in my noon-cells
                          all hail thee
and the village milk-maids
                    in my marrow
                          all hail thee
and the leap-year dancers
                    in my hair
                          all hail thee
and the hoi poloi in my loins all crave thee
holy holy earthy glory;
                    AVE VALERIE . . ! AVE VALERIE . . . !
                          (Lorgorligi, pp. 126–8)
```

Sometimes Okai's imagery is stark naked and shocks with its unchecked eroticism:

```
       I
shall cause
```

To be sculptured
I
shall cause
To be erected,
   A phallus-erect
   Marble-granite
 Totem
   Right into the naked navel
Of the virgin open – ocean:
       (Oath, pp. 135–6)

This type of imagery is not limited to his love poems. Some of the others with much more serious and lofty themes are also marked by this fondness for the erotic. 'Rhododomdroms in Donkeydom', the title piece of a forthcoming volume, opens with an account of the creation of the world as given in Yoruba mythology. The great creation myth is presented as a sexual drama which opens with 'two hands spreading a woman's thighs apart', and the arrival of Oduduwa (the god of creation) is announced in terms suggestive of the climax to a sexual act.

However, love and sex are not Okai's basic preoccupation. He is first and foremost a poet with a definite social call. In a recent symposium on 'The African writer and his society' held at Legon, Okai made this point clear when he declared that 'in Africa, the poet cannot afford to just play around with words. It is natural that he should handle some of the realities of his society.' This is what he seeks to do in most of his poems. The very choice of title poems for his volumes is indicative of his acceptance of this responsibility. In 'The Oath of the Fontomfrom' we see the poet's role in the symbolism of the primal drum, the focal point of a society's communal will to live in spite of enemies.

  Yet they shall seek
      after me –
 They shall seek to break
      my neck,
 Bury me
   alive
     massacre my children
 And squeeze me
     into a bottle.

The poet is sought because the enemies of his people know that

  when you want to starve
      the ocean,
 You paralyse
   its source,
     the river,

and because he has 'torn down the mask from the faces of our ill-wishers'. But like the chief-priest, he accepts his heavy responsibility with good-will. He will carry the burden of his people, still 'proud and even strengthened that they aim at [him]'. He is the source of inspiration and 'a voice of vision':

> Let no hand carve
> >   our tombstone
> Now . . .
> >   we have already in our time,
> Out-lived
> >   the sharpness of the sword,
> The din of the struggle,
> >   the clashes of cutlasses;
> We shall yet outlive
> >   the weight
> >   of lead.
>
> >   (*Oath*, p. 19)

In 'Lorgorligi Logarithms' the poet takes us into the complicated realms of what he once called 'the arithmetic of life'. *Lorgorligi*, we learn, is a Ga picture word for that which is 'meandering, labyrinthine, zigzag, something that is not straight'. First, the poet calls on several people, friends as well as enemies, to come witness how

> the quantum physics of existential
> inequality
> blows up the dorkordiki bowl of human
> sanity.
> >   (*Lorgorligi*, p.13)

Several things do not go straight with our world. For twelve years out of seventeen the heart of Seth Solomon Asare Bonsu did not beat smoothly, 'due to circumstances beyond our control', and now he has 'obeyed the temporal laws of gravity'. Three years ago, the poet arrived here in Ghana, 'hoping he had come, believing he had landed', but it was in the wrong season. The intelligence service people discovered that he was from a country

> with which our masters in the west
> were not
> on Ayeeko terms (ha! ha! ha!).

So they took his passport, re-stamped it and put him back on the next plane

> to a western port of entry where I would be
> quarantined and where my whole mind would be
> properly disinfected with our master's almighty
> izal and dettol.

Here Okai is re-enacting his own story of how after graduating with an MA (Litt.) from the Gorky Literary Institute in Moscow, he had to be sent to London to take an M.Phil, in Russian Literature in order to properly qualify for a lectureship in the University of Ghana where he now teaches. If the world were not 'lorgorligi', this would not have happened to him.

Both Apronti[5] and Dseagu[6] have rightly drawn attention to Okai's constant dwelling on the tragic side of life. The title poems of his two forthcoming volumes confirm this. 'Rhododomdroms in Donkeydom' deals with the worries of an artist, the creator, operating within a broken-down social order. As Okai himself explains, it is about 'beautiful flowers in a kingdom of fools'. The other volume, 'The Gong-Gongs of Mount Gontimano', promises to take us back to another version of the poet's social role. Here, he is no longer the communal drum, but a town-crier with an iron bell, shouting himself hoarse from the mountain top. By implication, the message must be urgent and crucial, a further development in the 'lorgorligi logarithms' of life. However, although he has a fondness for tragic themes, Okai's point of view is not necessarily 'more pessimistic than optimistic', as Dseagu suggests. He is a man with a healthy respect for life and he confronts the problems of the world without sounding apologetic about even his failures. He loves to dramatize the pain being inflicted on him, but he does not bemoan his plight:

> You are stepping upon my raw eggs – [testicles?]
> You are stepping upon my raw eggs
> and Jesus wept . . . but I shall not.
>
> (*Oath*, p. 82)

Okai spares himself the weakness of self-pity:

> You spoil my market,
> You walk on my green grass,
> And of course, I am not complaining
> You ask my name twice
> You muffle my chant
> And of course, I am not complaining.
>
> (*Oath*, p. 95)

He may not complain, but he often warns and threatens, as is seen in these lines from 'Afadzato' which at once impress with the forthrightness of the poet and the boldness of his imagery:

> I am a hangman . . .
> I enjoy hanging . . .
> But only with a clear conscience . . . if standing
> on my testicles you see me still quiet, do

not think me dumb or blind or dead . . . I
am merely taking my time to make
sure it is my testicles and not my
toes you are standing upon . . . I
am merely taking my time to make
sure exactly who it is standing
on my testicles . . . for I hate to hand
the innocent . . .
                                                          (*Oath*, p. 94)

Even in the most hopeless moments when

survival is slippery
the human head
is weighed down with the pressure
of tears   (*Lorgorligi*, p. 49)

the poet's indomitable spirit soars above the skies, assuring the world:

Let no hand carve
                                 our tombstone
Now . . .
               we shall refuse to die!
Our dove
            shall fly
                          across the flames
Of the big bonfires
                             of time –
But her feathers
                        shall stay unburnt.   (*Oath*, p. 20)

A mood of resolute defiance runs through Okai even in his most tragic
moments. It constitutes a point of equi-balance to what might otherwise
have been a negative view of life. 'Lorgorligi Logarithms', for all its
dwelling on the tragic, ends on a note of triumph. The poet had earlier
diagnosed his society's malady:

my motherland's nose, TAFLATSE, is running
et cetera
and god where are you, et cetera
our tap-root TAFLATSE is all rotten
and all we do is follow TAFLATSE any fool
                                                          (*Lorgorligi*, p. 24)

One would have thought that with their tap-root all rotten the people
must be heading for an inevitable collapse. But the poet soon transforms
our lament into shouts of victory:

woman! woman!
how often you carry the heaviness
of your soul . . . only to empty it into songs . . .

though our dialectic has been arrested
and frozen in mid-season
yet the algebra of the revolution
is being worked out . . .

and one of these days I am going
to make you
my kingmaker

le peuple; oui! the masses, yes!

(*Lorgorligi*, p. 51)

Closely linked with this spirit of defiance, a keen sense of humour runs through Okai's poems. Sometimes it is enough for him to just sit back and, with good-humoured contempt, reflect upon the foolishness of a world in which 'tomatoes are envying potatoes'. Such a world must be coming to an end, but the poet is too amused to grieve; he only needs to take note of these things and move on:

I shall put a pipe to my lips
And allow the tobacco-coated smoke

To ascend with the redigested memories
That refuse to fade away . . .

(*Oath*, p. 96)

Okai's sense of humour is often at work even when he is most serious. Where it succeeds, it has the effect of taking the bite off the unpleasant truths placed before us. Thus in the following lines, our attention is quickly shifted from the misery of the hunchback to the hurried flight of a man haunted by his own conscience:

the hunchback hums a hymn you
happen to know and suddenly
you decide you are in a hurry

(*Lorgorligi*, p. 34)

Okai sometimes over-indulges his sense of humour and makes one feel cheated. It is as if a man comes to you with tears in his voice, and when you begin to lament with him, he suddenly breaks into laughter. This is what happens, for instance, in 'Adikanfo' when at a particularly solemn moment in our lament for young Bonsu, we are unexpectedly introduced to the image of the rainbow urinating upon us:

your dew turns its back on our dawn
are we to look for your smile in the lightning
the rainbow pees upon our peace.

                                                         (*Lorgorligi*, p. 15)

One very interesting aspect of Okai's sense of humour may be seen in
his various presentations of the image of God. His god is a very fascinat-
ing version of the almighty Creator-God. He is certainly an artist with a
gift for perfection (as seen at work in 'Flowerfall'), but above all he is very
human, alive, and extremely practical, even if quite overwhelmed by his
responsibilities. In 'Modzawe' (*Oath*, pp. 126–7) we meet God in the
flesh. He is a patriarch and has woken up at dawn to have a bath before
sunrise. He has a bath towel thrown over his shoulder and is walking
briskly 'to the rising sun's river-sea'. Suddenly he is confronted by one of
his great-grandchildren who has a complaint to make. There is something pathetic in both the physical and emotional state of this great-
grandchild:

I shall step into his way, and
Planting my one one-quarter feet
Firmly upon the feeble earth,
I shall weep the hell world out
Of my inside and thereafter shout:
Someone has stolen away
My great grandmother's bones!
Let human beings be human beings again
Let human beings be human beings again
Let human beings be human beings again

In 'Invocation' (*Oath*, p. 74) God assumes the image of a busy elec-
tronics operator at the control tower of a gigantic communications net-
work. He is quite agitated because the switchboard is jammed and there
is a breakdown in communication between heaven and earth and some
men on earth are forcing words into God's mouth. In 'Dedication' (p. 73)
the picture is even bolder. We are warned not to 'start hurling blocks
towards the heavens',

. . . for even God in his
chambers, squatting in his
hyena skin pajamas has not
finished signing all his third
party insurance papers.

These unusual images of God form part of a major characteristic of
Atukwei Okai's craft. In the use of imagery he has a preference for the
dramatic. He is not given to painting still-life. His is a universe of great
energy and constant motion, often bordering on a clash of wills but never

degenerating into chaos. Even Okai's love passion in 'Dreamdom Communique To Valerieville' is realized in the images of prairie fires, honey hunters, night antelopes, tornado silences, village milkmaids, leap-year dancers, dawn detonators and Kikuyuyan hyenas. In 'Evesong in Soweto' a man stands accused by his own conscience and we see him as a tragic hero in a little dramatic sketch:

> when your conscience takes
> a penalty kick against the
> goal of your deeds and dreams
> you may leave behind
> the same old lord
> and the same old god
> the same old gong
> the same old song
>
> only send me
>
> another dream
>
> a different dream

(Lorgorligi, p. 58)

Another poem in which we find an unusual dramatic use of imagery is '999 Smiles' (*Oath*, pp. 38–41) which tells the pathetic story of two great friends who have fallen out. One finds himself 'perched' on top of the world, but he is not content with just looking down upon those below. Rather he chooses to worsen their misery by throwing stones at them. His one-time friend's misery is intensified by the knowledge that he cannot even react in self-defence, for his brother has taken the precaution of stealing away his only weapon, his hands. But what pains him most is that not so long ago they were such great friends, fully agreed on several truths of life. The extent of their friendship and agreement is presented in an unforgettable metaphor which opens the poem:

> nine hundred and ninety-nine smiles
> plus
> one quarrel ago, our eyes and our
> hearts
> were in agreement full

and the pain is effectively registered by the lines reiterating the betrayer's criminal act of

> hurling . . .
>
> stones . . .

                                    at us . . .

            infernal . . .

                      stones . . .
                                    at us . . .

        sinister . . .

                  stones . . .

                              at us . . .

Contrasting with this type of imagery developed into dramatic sketches
are other examples suggestive of the quiet and tender side of things, as in
'Adikanfo' where the poet announces his second homecoming 'from the
doldrums' and tells us:

> I am manuring my memory into
> a fertile remembrance of things recent and past

and in 'Kperterkple Serenade' where his tenderness is seen in the image
of a sunrise:

> with the politeness of a sunrise I knock
> upon your door
> but you do not want to know
> peace
> unto your ashes

Atukwei Okai's poetry deserves attention. There is great originality in
his approach, though as often happens with men who choose to go their
own way, there are moments of failure. The successes, where they do
come, are of great significance. The man Oshamraku Atukwei, organ-
grinder to God and man, has recorded a plea for remembrance which we
should take note of:

> And when they ask who the hell I was
> and what the hell on earth
>   I did, remind them I cared
>   enough to rise at dawn and
>   roll my mat, and that I, too, during
>   the festival of the soul, sang our
>   world.

                                                          (*Oath*, p. 119)

References

1. John Okai, *Oath of the Fontomfrom and Other Poems* (New York, Simon & Schuster, 1971), p. 75. The other collection of Okai's poetry discussed in this essay is *Lorgorligi Logarithms* (Tema, Ghana Publishing Corporation, 1974).
2. K. K. Dei-Annang, 'Discipline in the making of poetry', *Universitas*, II, 1 (1972), p. 115.
3. A. Irele, 'The criticism of modern African literature', in C. Heywood (ed.), *Perspectives on African Literature* (London, Heinemann, 1972), p.20.
4. Donatus Nwoga, Annual Report on West Africa, *Journal of Commonwealth Literature* (December 1974), p. 37.
5. 'John Atukwei Okai: the growth of a poet', *Universitas*, II, 1 (1972), p. 124.
6. In his Introduction to *Lorgorligi Logarithms*, p. xix.

6
'The Colour of Truth':
Lenrie Peters and African Politics

▼▼▼▼▼▼▼▼▼▼▼▼▼▼▼▼▼▼▼▼▼▼▼▼▼▼▼▼

ROMANUS N. EGUDU

'AFRICA has slept too long at the geographical centre of the world, a mere plaything eternally castrated', Lenrie Peters has written. 'She has observed much folly and has yet to reclaim her birthright of authority'.[1] African politics is one of the preoccupations of Peters's poetry; and he does not mind being 'run . . . through/with odiousness, Politics/Isms, deceits, vanities', provided he is left with 'the colour of truth'.[2] This truth is about the African colonial experience, independence, political leadership and the cure for her political ills. Peters proceeds from diagnosis to prescription and believes that the African must recognize himself for what he really is – a being whose soul has been bruised by the colonialists, neo-colonialists and African politicians – before he can redeem himself.

Peters considers the change brought about by colonialism in Africa unwelcome. Specifically the change, as we learn in the poem 'Home Coming' (*Satellites*, p. 39), consists in 'the present' which

> . . . reigned supreme
> Like the shallow floods over the
> gutters
> Over the raw paths where we had been
> The house with the shutters.

It also embraces the 'cultivated weeds' which have grown 'where we led/The virgins to the water's edge', and that 'house without a shadow/ Lived in by new skeletons'. The images of 'shallow floods', 'weeds' and 'skeletons' adequately point out the flimsiness and worthlessness of the change that has been forced on the people. The essential contrast in this poem is between the richness of what is natural and the impotence of what is artificial. It is this disparity between the new and the old which is more harassing to the poet than the contrast observed by Wilfred Cartney:

> Peters' poems 'Home Coming' and 'We Have Come Home' are not jubilant songs celebrating the homecoming; but ones in which, through the contrast of exile and return, of deception and promise, the poet evokes the pathos of homecoming, the resilience of the spirit that comes back to the 'green foothills' of Africa.[3]

For instance, the 'raw paths' have been replaced by what Kofi Awoonor calls the 'flimsy glories of paved streets'.[4] And the 'new skeletons' are part of the 'present' because they are the home-made representatives of the departed colonialists; they are in fact the African politicians who, as we shall see later, lack all substance.

While 'Home Coming' deals with physical change, 'We Have Come Home'[5] is about spiritual and psychological change: but both types of change are for the worse. In the latter poem, the harm done by colonialism is the worse; in spite of the fact that 'our boots [are] full of pride', we come 'with sunken hearts' and experience the 'true massacre of the soul'; we are 'loved' apparently by the colonial masters, yet we are not 'left alone'; though we have come home, we are singing songs of other lands; and our fate is determined not by us, but by the masters who apply the mechanical and chance method of 'spinning' a coin. After the colonial experience what we have left are famine, drought and the 'sodden spirit' which supports 'the tortured remnants/of the flesh'. The truth is that in the end the African is left without 'dignity'.

Another dimension of change, more painful because it touches the very roots of the people's being, is symbolized by the axe of colonialism which has fallen on Katchikali, the Gambian god of fertility, procreation and protection. The sacred grove of this god is at Bakau, a village where Peters lives, directly behind his residence as if for immediate protection. Its totem is the crocodile. Every year the people appease the god in a special ceremony, during which the men pray for rich harvest, and sterile women pray for children. In the title poem,[6] the mysteries of Katchikali are undermined by the élite, the products of colonialism. Their ancestors, as if held by 'magic spells', worshipped the god with humility; the 'crocodiles/of another world/under your waters' were 'tame as pumpkins'; 'the women weight-drowned/towards the farms bend/their knees and say a prayer' to Katchikali; 'lovers under a fertile moon/pray for their children', and

> Old men sing songs
> When the moon is high;
>   pray for their crops
> and homes though they be warrens.

But faith in Katchikali has given way to disrespect towards him, by the 'new people' who do not understand him and 'would ignore your mysteries'. Now 'all the institutions crumble':

> As the mud hut crumbles
> withers, all is base
> seething self-interest and corruption
> and the demon of gain
> in your waters Katchikali.

Hunters kill the god's totems, the crocodiles, for meat and hide, and fish in his waters. In retaliation, the god appears to have abandoned his votaries:

> . . . your wisdom is silent.
> we call to you
> there are no answers.
> We reach out to you
> beyond ineffable darkness

Ships no longer hastily pass by the waters of Katchikali in dread, 'but belch warm welcomes in the night/against the quivering gates/of the new cities of the plain'. Thus the god is totally destroyed, together with the cultural heritage of the people which he represents.

The nature of Africa's loss as a result of colonization is also highlighted in Peters's lone novel, *The Second Round*, where we find the following reflection:

> The African did not know what was to become of him. Unwittingly, he had bartered his soul for material gain. He had lost a good deal of his heritage in the process, yet had not been fully admitted into the closely-guarded traditions of his rulers.[7]

Whatever material gain the African realized from his contact with the West is offset by his loss of dignity, even of his humanity. This is what should be recovered by independent Africa. But as Peters sees it, the truth behind African independence is as painful as that of the colonial experience. In 'Where Are the Banners Now'[8] he shows independence to be paradoxical from the outset; the banners of freedom are stained 'with blood from the lacerated womb'; the slogans which 'disfigured the alien face' also 'cut in pieces' the African children whose 'cries will still be heard tomorrow'; and the flags designed 'to mark/The death of our recent history' are flown at half-mast as if there were 'death in the land'. The disquiet all over the land points to the ineffectiveness of independence:

Who will climb into the broad plains
Where they can see the tattered crowd
Women beating their heads in sorrow
Because their men are made impotent with
    guilt?
Who will look down from the Eagle's crater
Secured inside the solid rock
And bring us the Tablets yet again
On which the promises and the Law stand out
    in gold?

Post-colonial Africa is not only economically dependent on the former and other masters, but is also riddled with social discrimination and injustice. Peters thoroughly diagnoses Africa's impotence in 'In the Beginning'[9] and concludes that only sincere and selfless unity could save the continent. The poet compares the glorious and purposeful beginning of the struggle for independence, marked by 'one voice', 'one cry' and 'one promise', with the gloomy present, marked by the deceit, arrogance and selfishness of the politicians. Early in the struggle the leaders with their emphasis on 'unity', 'the word/which crazed and touched the sky', won the hearts of the people. Everybody was involved:

Each man in his heart
with a wish, a vote
with brawn and elbow grease
played his part.
The peasant in the field
the clerk
the labourer with his sack
bowed heads to the tool in hand
raised voices to the sky.
Freedom, unity, prosperity
We shall abolish
the Tse-Tse fly.

The people's total commitment became complete frustration when their leaders turned misleaders and oppressors. For shortly after the attainment of independence, the leaders started begging 'in style'; they wanted to 'change the face of the Continent' with 'industrial development/Dams, factories' before providing such basic needs as shelter and education for the poor and their children.

Peters traces the continuing poverty and social injustice on the continent to lack of political unity. The Organization of African Unity which could save the continent from poverty and foreign exploitation is ineffective, for several reasons. First, the neo-colonialists discourage unity: 'As for unity/go have your heads examined/What do you want it for?'

Secondly, the African countries are not prepared to help one another:

> Let each look to himself –
> that's what the white man taught
> us, be content
> we earned our Independence
> Let South Africa do the same.

This selfishness is in the tradition of the 'divide and rule' device by which white imperialism was fostered on the continent. Thirdly, African leaders lack faith in unity; each wants to be the leader of Africa and is not interested in unity based on equality. As a result, Africa remains a plaything, like a football, passed on by white imperialism to 'yellow imperialism' and then, ironically, to black imperialism. Peters's seriousness is reinforced by his colloquial tone; the 'tragedy' is presented in a comic form to ridicule the architects of the African inertia.

Edwin Thumboo has observed: 'In *Satellites* the poems on broad African themes are underwritten. They are not undertaken with Peters's characteristic utterance and merely confirm that the subject had little to move him. Perhaps Africa as a subject proves too large unless personalized.'[10] It is, of course, not true that Africa as a subject does not move Peters. Rather, he appears so oppressed by the ugly experience that he forgets artifice and concentrates on the matter. While it can be accepted that a poem like 'In the Beginning' does not reflect Peters's characteristic powerful imagery and diction, it has its own peculiar artistic beauty arising from its dramatic, comic and colloquial qualities. The true nature of Africa's plight is brought out effectively by the African voices heard all through the poem.

Peters insists that Africans must face the reality of their situation. This is why in 'You talk to me of "self" ' (*Katchikali*, no. 63) he directs our attention to the inner chambers of that reality:

> Go into villages, not palaces;
> Look among goats and sheep
> under pyramids of squalor
> degradation, the moon's eclipse . . .
>
> There is your 'Self' crushed
> between the grinding wheel
> of ignorance and the centuries;
> the blood congealed in the baking sun.

This is the real Africa, quite different from the 'African beauty/The chocolate icing and Mascara "selves"/along the ports and river's edge' which 'Senghor extols'. In all his poems about Africa Peters endeavours to throw off the masks with which Africans have camouflaged their true

selves, so that they could see themselves for what they are – the unde-
veloped members of the human family – and consequently rouse themselves from centuries of slumber. In contrast, African politicians spend
their time and talent on destructive projects, such as organizing *coups
d'état*. 'It is time for reckoning Africa' (*Katchikali*, no. 64) is a serious
indictment of the lack of unity of purpose among African leaders. They
sit on 'wicker thrones/ghosted by White ants', while the internal birds of
prey 'live on the fat of the land'.

> all threatening coups
> and claiming vast receipts
> like winsome children
> feeding on mother's milk.

And those 'who tell the biggest lies' get the biggest reward. This is all the
more frustrating for the poet because as these 'vultures feed on
sturgeon's eggs', the few honest men 'stand/waiting at the door/or rot
in prison cells'. He therefore appeals to this continent 'of great hopes/and
boundless possibilities' to become alert to her predicament, and not to
mind 'New York' or 'America'. For now is 'the lost time/and future time'
to end all revolutions and make a 'straight path/from world to better
world'.

Peters considers African politicians the continent's greatest enemy
because of their insincerity, ignorance, violence and indolence. In
poem after poem we find unsavoury images of the politician. In 'The
Man on the Podium' (*Katchikali*, no. 44), the politician is presented as a
'hollow shrill creature' who 'barks' and whose 'searchlight eyes blanket
the audience/but do not penetrate'; he is 'this significantly empty/sad
fellow'. In 'Plea to Mobutu' (*Katchikali*, no. 45), the implacable violence
of the politician is depicted:

> This vile contemptible game of politics
>   since it must be played
> let it be mellowed with compassion,
>   justice, effect
> Tshombe's death won't bring you heaven,
>   or respect,
> only the vacant clap of thunder,
>   rifle butt
> on skull from feud to feud assail
>   on bloody
> oceans, where violence annihilates
>   the good.

This 'plea' is addressed not only to Mobutu but to all those African
leaders who, during the Congo crisis of the 1960s, opposed Tshombe's

return to the country. Elsewhere, Peters had stated that 'the comedy of errors of the Congo affair' constituted a forum for the demonstration of 'African disunity and even fear of unity'.[11] What pained him most about the Congo crisis was the African leaders' disregard for a major African philosophy of life, that whenever the eyes weep, the nose also weeps in sympathy; for people should be as organically related as the various parts of the body are related to one another. This disregard for physical and moral cohesion is not only unnatural but also suicidal, since it has exposed various parts of Africa to the murderous intervention of foreign powers.

Peters sees the African leaders' attitude to the Congo crisis as a specimen of their unresponsiveness to change. They seem unprepared to learn from past experience, as the contrast between nature and man in 'The rasping winds lash with demented strings' (*Katchikali*, no. 59) clearly shows. Here, the active and fruitful awakening of nature is contrasted with the languid and passive awakening of Africa:

> The rasping winds lash with demented
>   strings
> their old protagonist earth from
>   antique sleep
> the tearful trees unbend from
>   ritual dance
> and shake their heads and stand
>   erect . . .
>
> Africa awakes to new beginnings, preens
>   her head
> like nourished blades of grass forced
>   out of earth
> a distant inch or two while you observe
> their lush, erotic smiles of sobering death.

Even the African soil, heavy with promise, the ancestral spirits that should protect the living, and the sky that is 'hot-rimmed crimson with hell flames' which should rouse people from sleep – these are 'kindly silent like some thrones of kings'. In the face of stresses the African woodsman is about his business, the women pound 'corn along the path', and the men are 'wrestling, gesticulating, falling and rising in prayer/ with face sublime and heads besmirched with dust/like mystic, anguished scenes of lust'. The problems confronting Africa cannot be solved by such dreamy 'gesticulations', but have to be faced with purposeful action. That is why life must take up 'her cudgels once again' to lash the indolent into consciousness of desired response. The African should learn from the weaver-birds in 'The weaver-birds are nesting'

(*Katchikali*, no. 60). The hippos and the crocodiles sleep all day, but the weaver-birds nest and sing 'from dawn till evening/and next morning, they're first to wake'. Owing to their lethargy African politicians have kept the continent down by failing to provide the basic amenities. In the highly dramatic poem, 'Waking in the Night' (*Katchikali*, no. 69), we see the enraged physician who receives a message: 'If you're not asleep, please come at once.' But because he has to grope in the dark for his equipment, it is dawn when he finally emerges from the room, by which time it is too late to save the life he is called upon to save. The doctor's rage will yield no results:

> You swear an instant letter to the
> Minister
> We must have light, electric light
> each minute of the day and night
>
> A dismal six months later
> you're still groping in the dark
> the difference is, it has become a
> way of life.

The image of Africa presented in the poetry of Lenrie Peters is one of disunity, political instability, social injustice and basic under-development. But he makes a number of recommendations to improve the situation. To reorder her society, Africa needs ideas from all over the world. Peters advises her to

> Open the gates
> To East and West
> Bring in all
> That's good and best.[12]

Africa should welcome from every quarter of the globe people who bring ideas for her development, and absorb their gifts as earth does 'the new rain/Which washes away the tears/And the sweat stain'. Peters firmly believes that the development of Africa largely depends on her ability to learn from other people and from history. 'The African', he has written, 'must broaden his soul to comprehend all, yet retain the tint of his skin with dignity, and he must learn from the mistakes of history.'[13] He goes on to emphasize that Africa cannot afford to be isolated from the rest of the world:

> If Africa can be more rapidly developed by closely associating with the West, then she must temporarily swallow her pride and do so . . . Non-alignment for its own sake and as an exhibition of political arrogance is obsolete. The course of the world is set in the direction of alignments, and Africa must realize this and accept it.[14]

While posing such an association as a pragmatic solution to Africa's problems of underdevelopment, Peters does not see Africans as passive beneficiaries of other people's thoughts. Rather, they must do their own thinking, and use borrowed thoughts only for the purpose of reinforcing their own. In other words the basic ideas which Africa needs for her development should be generated by Africans. It is perhaps for this reason that Peters advises 'steady reacquaintance' with the past, in his poem of that title.[15] The 'vast consciousness of the past' carries 'a voice of steel/and channels like hardened arteries' which 'can absorb a part of this despair/Of flesh and mind'. The present despair can be turned to hope in future only on the basis of solid ideas to be yielded by the African tradition:

> The Grid survives in sustentacular
> Protuberance with stores of current
> To light our way at the turning of a screw.

The insistence is on light, on the thinking mind which produces ideas. The African past is seen as a vast reservoir of electric light, which can be switched on as soon as the necessary contact is assured. The electricity image not only implies illumination, but also power and precision of effect.

However, there is an aspect of Africa's past which Peters would like to see discarded and forgotten. This is the colonial past. It should be forgotten because Peters believes that continued pining over the pain it caused will distract us from the essential search for a new and enduring order of existence. In 'How do we come with rage?' (*Katchikali*, no. 19), he discourages all forms of grief and sentimentality; instead, he encourages Africans to embrace the 'new dawn'. Instead of singing, like Negritude poets, 'songs of shame/Searching the inner blackness/where healthy plants replace/The burnt-out embers of hate', or journeying to 'the centre of the earth', which symbolizes darkness, 'when all is outward spreading/Along untrodden path', they should sing of a reborn Africa which has shed her 'black cloak' and nobly bears the 'grace of suffering':

> . . . offers herself
> Her love for hate
> Peace for war
> Dignity for alien savagery.

Ideas are the chief means of effecting this transformation, and they must be given free play after the experience of the 'bitter storm' of colonialism. Peters strongly believes that one of Africa's most serious problems is her lack of ideas, and he feels that Africans, like the Chinese, must do their own thinking, if they are to be free. But the over-riding need is for unity which Peters considers an urgent desideratum for African salvation. He believes that only an unequivocal and sovereign unity will provide a lasting solution to Africa's problems. This unity will enable Africa 'externally to stand against a world of troubles, and by contending end them'; and 'internally to increase the prosperity of every citizen down to the most rural peasantry and to bring to each existence a fullness of life'.[16] Peters's humanism is directed towards the welfare of the poor in the African society. Thus the 'united Africa' of his vision is one 'which will better provide what many separate states cannot or will not provide: health, food, employment, education, housing, law and order, confidence and abolition of fear; and will provide it for all with equal competence and dedication'.[17]

Peters has given poetic expression to these thoughts. For example, in 'There will be time for homecoming' (*Katchikali*, no. 42), he exhorts unity once the battle is won against external and internal divisive elements. After the killing of the snake coiled 'under the pillow', the laying down of 'bayonets' and the outlawing of 'the coarse barbaric/slash of panga knives', there will be time

> . . . to take a fellow
>   by the shoulder saying
> 'we two are common citizens
> without tribe, caste, nation, race
>   without the mischievous
>   cloak of fiscal shrouds'
> Time to dip clean fingers
>   in the bowl together
> Unity of God.

The 'Unity of God' is metaphysical, embracing all humanity; as such, there will be time for it. But the unity of Africa, which should be its prelude, is more urgent. For this unity 'there is not enough time', for the 'sea encroaches' and the 'poison' of hostility spreads. The poet prays for unity because he knows that otherwise the future will be bleak. Unity, like all treasures, is hidden in a difficult environment – 'Under the throbbing stone' – and it will take hard work to acquire it. Thus 'we need the eagerness', according to the poem of that title,[18] of 'children to listen/learn, reflect as/well as for milk', if we must achieve this unity. We also need 'solid self-reliance' which is 'worth more than votes' for 'integration' which makes for 'greatness' is indispensable to the existence of Africa. There is, here, a lesson to be learnt from nature:

Flesh and red clay
alike comprehend
the futility of
dissociation.

In moving from the reality of diagnosis to the idealism of prescription, Peters's dream of creating a united continent from the present African nations ignores the fact that because Africa is linked with the rest of the world economically, politically and ideologically, she has to contend with forces working against the creation of her continental sovereignty. However, his suggestion that Africans must do their own thinking and develop the quality of self-reliance in order to become completely independent is most timely, as is also his plea that priority attention should be paid to the provision of social amenities for all classes of people, especially those in rural areas; for the poor living conditions in African villages belie Africa's claims to modernity.

Part of Peters's uniqueness lies in his comprehensive view of and concern about Africa. Of all modern African poets of English expression, he is the least concerned about his own country and most concerned about the fate of the continent as a whole. He considers himself first an African, and secondly a Gambian. Although Peters has not used the techniques of African oral literature, or African linguistic devices, his poems reflect the African spirit and sensibility in their handling of socio-political problems.

References

1. Lenrie Peters, 'Thoughts on unity', unpublished essay, 1976, p. 2.
2. Lenrie Peters, 'Skyflood of locusts', *Satellites* (London, Heinemann, 1967), pp. 1–3.
3. Wilfred Cartey, *Whispers from a Continent: The Literature of Contemporary Black Africa* (London, Heinemann, 1971), p. 214.
4. Kofi Awoonor, 'The Anvil and the Hammer', *Night of My Blood* (New York, Doubleday, 1971), p. 29.
5. *Satellites*, pp. 31–3.
6. 'Katchikali', *Katchikali* (London, Heinemann, 1971), no. 56. Further references to *Katchikali* will be inserted in the essay.
7. *The Second Round* (London, Heinemann, 1966), p. 103.
8. *Satellites*, pp. 97–8.
9. ibid., pp. 80–90.
10. Edwin Thumboo, 'The universe is my book: Lenrie Peters', *African Literature Today*, 6 (1973), p. 98.
11. Peters, 'Thoughts on unity', op. cit., p. 30.
12. *Satellites*, pp. 30–1.
13. Peters, 'Thoughts on Unity', op. cit., p. 34.
14. ibid., p. 38.
15. ibid., pp. 79–80.
16. ibid., p. 15.
17. ibid.
18. *Satellites*, p. 68.

7

The Duty of Violence in Yambo Ouologuem's *Bound to Violence*

▼▼▼▼▼▼▼▼▼▼▼▼▼▼▼▼▼▼▼▼▼▼▼▼▼▼▼▼▼▼

YUSUFU MAIANGWA

THIS is an attempt to analyse the now largely discredited novel *Bound to Violence*[1] by Yambo Ouologuem, by means of an investigative approach that seeks to establish the link between the structural and aesthetic construction of the novel on the one hand and the passage of certain semiotic signs on the other. This essay will try to answer one of the many legitimate questions that can be asked about literature. How and to what extent can we examine a novel like *Bound to Violence* from a semiological point of view without necessarily being too 'scientific' and without impairing its fundamental qualities as a work of art?

Practically all the major exponents of semiotics have applied their new science to literature. Roland Barthes, recently appointed to the Chair of Literary Semiotics at the prestigious Collège de France in Paris, has called semiology 'a part of linguistics, or, to be precise, that part which would take over the great *signifying units* of speech'.[2] If we take *Bound to Violence* to be a kind of *discours*, then what needs to be done is to analyse the 'signifying units' which critics have tended to ignore in their haste to lay emphasis on polemics. Barthes sees communication as a polarization of two signifying units: *denotation* and *connotation*. Indeed, these are two of the levels of communication constantly used in *Bound to Violence* to pinpoint those aspects that deal with the notion of violence as a means of achieving social and political goals. Buyssens has defined semiology as 'the study of the processes of communication, that is, of the means used to influence others, and recognized as such by the person one wishes to influence'.[3] Buyssens's 'signs' and Barthes's 'units' refer to the same thing. And it is important to note that definitions of semiotics are frequently based on this diachronic opposition between the cardinal concepts of sign and signal. Prieto, using Buyssens's works as the basis of his research, defines a sign as 'an immediate perceptible fact which makes us know something about another fact which is not perceptible'.[4] Buyssens himself says, on the nature of signals:

> The perceptible fact associated with a state of consciousness is realized voluntarily in order that the witness may recognize its destination . . . In short (as opposed to the sign) the signal is the act by which an individual, aware of a perceptible fact that is associated with a state of consciousness, realizes this fact in order that another individual may understand the aim of this behaviour and reconstitute in his own consciousness what is happening in that of the first individual.[5]

The distinction between sign (or index) and signal is important if one is to understand fully the role of the different semiotic categories that may be used to interpret a highly topical novel like *Bound to Violence*. For instance, are we to classify such topics as violence, sex, sadism and colonization all of which are much in evidence in the novel, as signs or signals? To the extent that the distinction between a sign and a signal can be used to explain vital social and political phenomena, one is justified in saying that a sign is the external manifestation of an inward realization of the significance of any given phenomenon. An example from *Bound to Violence* will make this point clearer. The dogs Dick and Medor which the colonial administrator, Chevalier, uses to enhance his sexual pleasure are pure indices or signs at the outset. They are simply ferocious dogs. But the author also uses them to draw our attention to something other than mere dogs. Through a process of mental metamorphosis, the dogs cease momentarily to be dogs and become identified with Awa, the girl sent to Chevalier by Saif, although the colonial administrator does not know who sent her nor why she is there. The dogs become identified especially with her private parts and the pleasure she gives Chevalier:

> Her fingers under her armpits, she arched her back and screamed, feeling against her lips the rasping pungency of Dick's muzzle, while Chevalier grimacing relaxed his caressing of her loins and like a sticky cudgel Medor's hard, pointed tongue explored her vulva. (p. 57)

At other moments, the signs Dick and Medor are associated with the legs of a fleeing thief (in spite of the sort of exercises they indulge in, the dogs are still capable of chasing a thief!) or with a buck during a hunting expedition. Nevertheless, the transformation of Dick and Medor into signals is associated with new spacio-temporal circumstances – with France, for instance, and the sort of things Chevalier used to do there. It is only logical to suppose that since Chevalier is from Europe, this must be one of the 'bizarre' sexual practices that obtain there. From this realization to an outright moral condemnation of Chevalier is a step which the reader is invited to take. Thus, it is quite evident from the foregoing that one of the ways in which communication, via semiotic categories, can be established is to transform signs into signals and then leave the reader to draw his own conclusions. In *Bound to Violence*, symbols, metaphors, linguistic and non-linguistic sign-systems are all closely woven and built into the structure of the novel. This structure is so compact and yet so flexible that communication and meaning are interpretable quantities which ought to be examined critically and in such a manner as to reveal the necessity of the dialectical resolution of the forces and contradictions in which violence is the chief element.

When *Bound to Violence* was first published in 1968, it was highly praised in Europe and America. However, it was received with mixed feelings in Africa. Ouologuem was hailed by non-Africans as the first African intellectual of international standing since Senghor. Speaking to journalists in France, he claimed that his book spoke of leaders who posed as 'bawling revolutionaries while opening their tattered purses to capitalism'. He concluded: 'My aim is to do violence to the misconceptions of Africans so that we can realize what the real problems are. This is "our duty of violence".'[6] This duty is necessitated by the need to reformulate the philosophies on which the African society is based, in view of centuries of brutalization through a three-pronged act of violence – slave-trading activities from the north and south, internecine wars and razzias and colonization – which has created a new breed of humiliated Africans whom Ouologuem refers to in the novel as 'the nigger-trash'. His duty of violence is based not on physical violence, for Africans have surfeited themselves with that, but on intellectual violence, a sort of brainstorming aimed at making the people aware of the necessity for revolutionary change.

Bound to Violence is, of course, full of physical violence, and some of it does not appear to be serving any useful purpose. However, an act of violence that looks gratuitous may be utilized politically by someone else. For instance, Awa, who is treated by Chevalier as a pure object of sexual satisfaction, is murdered by her real lover, Sankolo, apparently because she catches him masturbating while watching Shrobenius's daughter, Sonia, fornicating with Saif's eldest son, Madoubo. 'Sankolo seized Awa by the throat. His knife whirled, twice he planted it in her breast, slitted her belly from top to bottom' (p. 93). As a result, Sankolo is banished. But Saif further exploits the situation:

> Saif . . . shrewd ideologist that he was, raised (to avenge himself for
> the scandal created by the murder of Awa) the prices on the Negro art

exchange, cooking up, to the sauce of tradition and its human values, a stew of pure symbolic religious art which he sent to Vandame, who passed it on to his correspondents who (may the Lord bless their innocence) peddled it to the curiosity seekers, tourists, foreigners, sociologists, and anthropology-minded Colonials who flocked to the Nakem. (p. 93)

Notice the transition from eroticism to death through violence undergone by Awa, and how the passage from one stage to another is consistently exploited by someone else. In addition, we are given all this in a jigsaw puzzle-like manner; and because the whole process is communicative, we are required to put the pieces together.

In one of his interviews with French journalists, Ouologuem admitted that his novel is negative, because it provides no solution to the problems, and that its only positive value is that it makes a fresh statement of the African reality. Actually, a novel can, at best, be only a guide on how to achieve political goals. In *Bound to Violence*, the process of putting the jigsaw pieces together is definitely a positive act, which may involve constant passage from one form of violence to another, and thereby give rise to the situation whereby violence often begets violence in the struggle for political and social independence.

In a review of the changing themes in the African novel, Abiola Irele has called attention to 'an entirely new kind of hero in the African novel, an individual who is realized almost wholly through the movements of his singular consciousness'. He illustrates his points by referring to three West African novels: Malick Fall's *La Plaie*, Kwei Armah's *The Beautyful Ones Are Not Yet Born* and *Bound to Violence*. He describes the last as the 'ultimate in the development of this sombre mood in the African novel', a 'meandering succession of sordid happenings, excesses and extravagances, presented as an historical narrative of a fictitious but "typical" African empire'.[7] Finally, Irele wonders whether Ouologuem's narrative does not hide some irony, whether the novel is not meant as a joke, a practical leg-pulling exercise. If the answer is in the affirmative, contends Irele, then the French reading public can sit back and watch the picture of Africa they have always wanted to see. If, however, Ouologuem has written his novel with his tongue in his cheek, then it is necessary to put the jigsaw pieces together, in order to interpret fully the significance and meaning of the novel. True, *Bound to Violence* does appear like 'a meandering succession of sordid happenings, excesses and extravagances'. But we must see this 'sordid' chain of events for what it really is. The events do not constitute an end in themselves; rather they are meant to catapult the reader into a new state of consciousness, to perceive the African reality in a new way. And the meandering is not so much in the cataloguing of sordid happenings as in the painstaking process whereby a certain vision of the African reality is communicated to us through a somewhat over-use of signs and symbols.

Mbelolo ya Mpiku, a Zaïrean critic, describes *Bound to Violence* as 'a sequence of violent acts, erotic deeds and unexpected turns of events' and dismisses the novel as a 'sure-fire formula of sex and violence'. He completely misses the point when he relegates *Bound to Violence* to the low status of a recipe for sex and violence, for he fails to see why these inseparable themes are built into the framework of the novel from the beginning to the end. Ignoring completely the inner dynamics of the composite themes of the novel that point to real political freedom, Mbelolo writes:

> Ouologuem's vision stands in contradiction with the African Reality . . . no African critic who loves his people and is proud of them can agree with Ouologuem's view that the Black man's predicament today is the result of an ontological flaw, an innate collective proclivity to slavery and spoliation, or an inveterate inability to work out adequate solutions for his own problems.[8]

Ouologuem is not saying that because the black man has been brutalized he has therefore acquired a propensity for violence and become incapable of providing adequate solutions to the numerous problems that beseige him. Rather, we should see the novel as an invitation to perform one more act of violence (intellectual, this time) in order to upset once and for all the oppressor's apple-cart. This important message is driven home through the alternate use of long and short sequences, which make us realize the importance of finding ways and means of getting out of our predicament.

It is pertinent to consider at this juncture the allegations of plagiarism which have been levied against Ouologuem. Most of them can in fact be used to assess the more positive virtues of the novel. In an article that was meant to be a tribute to the Black Arts Festival held in Lagos, Nigeria, early in 1977, Eric Sellin, an American critic, questioned Ouologuem's integrity:

> . . . We are not dealing with a forgery *à la* Brother Rowley or *à la* Vermeer but with a reliance on other writers' imaginative powers and a mechanical creative process which the author and the book itself (including the cover 'blurb') had at first led critics to take for a genuine impulse emanating from an individual talent and lending expression to the historico-ethnic heartbeat of a misunderstood continent. It is all well and good to eschew critical standards as outmoded and to main-

tain that art is solely in the eye of the beholder, but the fact remains
that a number of critics had felt that Ouologuem had enriched literature, not merely exploited or perpetrated it.[9]

This is another example whereby critics who once praised a 'best-seller'
for its originality have turned violently against it once its structural
affinities with existing works are 'discovered'. There is no instance in
literary history where a particular work has not in any way been influenced by another writer. Sellin cites André Schwarz-Bart's novel *Le
Dernier des justes* as the novel on which *Bound to Violence* is based. Neither
Ouologuem nor Schwarz-Bart denies this allegation; in fact, the latter
claims to be rather happy that his novel, which he compares to an
apple-tree, has been taken as the model for another work of art, and that
'his apples should be . . . taken and planted in another soil'.[10] True, the
forms of the two novels are identical, but their contents are radically
different.

The sheer beauty of Ouologuem's art deepens our perception of the
history of the blacks from about AD 1200 to the present day. His message
is that violence, in all its ramifications, is a necessary evil, if true and
lasting political freedom is to be achieved. Ouologuem uses the verb with
devasating effect, turning seemingly harmless transitives into ogres of
violence and action. The reader is inevitably drawn into a vortex of words
full of mystery, meaning and communication, right from the first paragraph of the novel:

> Our eyes drink the brightness of the sun and, overcome, marvel at
> their tears. *Mashallah! wa bismillah!* . . . To recount the bloody
> adventure of the niggertrash – shame to the worthless paupers! – there
> would be no need to go back beyond the present century; but the true
> history of the Blacks begins much earlier, with the Saifs, in the year
> 1202 of our era, in the African Empire of Nakem. (p. 3)

Like the griot or chronicler retelling for the umpteenth time the tribe's
history and explaining the more salient points of that history, Ouologuem sets off with lightning speed and draws us straight into a world of
blood and tears in which, from century to century, we see the Saifs,
rulers of Nakem, striving to aggrandize their empire or enrich themselves. Legends of the good and bad Saifs are used to describe events in
those centuries when the written tradition had not yet superseded the
oral. For instance, the legend of the good Saif Isaac al-Heit continues to
haunt 'Black romanticism and the political thinking of the notables in a
good many republics'. But Saif Isaac el-Heit's accursed son Saif al-
Haram and his minister 'spent large sums of money supporting the most
influential and discontented families at court . . . received bribes, pen-

sions, and titles of nobility as pompous as they are meaningless'. We are also told that their horses, to the number of 3260, drank milk in mangers inlaid with gold and ivory. 'Allah harmin Katamadjo!' (p. 11).

Another sequence captures, like the camera's eye, the niggertrash in their most humiliating moment, during the forcible journey from Africa to the Americas in which more than 100 million of them are involved. Once in their new 'homes' they face new problems which are not referred to explicitly but of which we are made aware through deductive reasoning. Here, the author uses violence and sex as the media of communication:

> Fascinated by the bodies of the slaves or by their quivering sex organs (it happened time and time again), a young girl whose beauty outmarveled her finery . . . would turn to her pink-and-white mother, if not for consolation then at least for a sign of interest or an authoritative opinion on black sexuality. One of the charming replies was: 'The Holy Father doesn't approve of *Café au Lait* . . .' (pp. 12–13).

Thus, moments of peace alternate with moments of violence and war, and each moment is a definite occasion to pass on a message with all its positive and negative aspects.

There is no denying the fact that the first part, subtitled 'The legend of the Saifs', is the backbone of the novel. All the sex and violence contained in the remaining three parts ('Ecstasy and Agony', 'The Night of the Giants' and 'Dawn') are referable to the first part. What the author is suggesting is that the quantity of violence and sex present in any society at any point in history is inversely proportional to the quality of government at that particular point in time. The crucial point is not that we blame those involved in this game of sex and violence but that we see how people indulge these passions with a view to rearranging the social and political order. So, when we read the following description of acts of sexual orgy and brutality, we are not unduly shocked. In his account of the ways Saif al-Haram encourages raids that refurbish the slave-ship, Ouologuem paints the stupor of the niggertrash of Saif's time and, vicariously, our own:

> The brains and the women's sexual parts were set aside for the 'eminent men'; with clearly aphrodisiac intent, the chief's testicles were sprinkled with pepper and strong spice, to be relished by the women in their communal soup. Ordained by hatred, innate evil, blood lust, thirst for vengeance, or perhaps by a desire to inherit the qualities of the devoured victims, the ghoulish feast ended in an orgy of drinking. (p. 16)

This sort of language is used to describe events in the Empire of

Nakem from the earliest times to about 1947. We are shown the various
ways in which sex and violence are exploited during the colonial days.
Every one uses violence to achieve his goals, Saif and the colonial
governors being the chief actors. The intellectual, Raymond Kassoumi,
a child of violence, comes to Paris for further studies and is inevitably
drawn into the hot vortex of sex and violence. He is typical of the young
men whom Saif deceives the white man into believing that he is educating
to serve the colonial cause; in reality, Saif sends them to Europe to learn
the white man's methods which they will later use against the white man.
According to the chronicler:

> The life that Raymond lived from that day on was the life of his whole
> generation – the first generation of native administrators maintained
> by the notables in a state of gilded prostitution – rare merchandise,
> dark genius manoeuvred behind the scenes and hurled into the tem-
> pests of colonial politics amidst the hot smell of festivities and machi-
> nations . . . (p. 136)

Colonial and, by implication, post-colonial politics are invariably
based on a substratum of violence, an acceptable weapon in the fight for
power. The *dabali* is the opium used by Saif and the colonial rulers to
subdue the people and make them perform all sorts of acts of violence.
Kassoumi mistakenly makes love to his own sister Kadidia in a group
orgy. But when he finally discovers the girl's identity, she tries to excuse
herself by explaining the situation at Nakem:

> I went to work as a servant for Jean-Luc Dalbard . . . Father worked
> there for six months without wages. Dalbard was supplied with *dabali*
> by Saif and Tal Idris. He mixed all sorts of stuff in the food to give the
> workers a hard on, so the poor bastards would work their balls off for
> more drugs and women . . . (pp. 145–6)

Kassoumi's revolt against the *status quo* is not taken seriously by the
authorities because it is intellectual and ineffective. All the same, he
reasons that if everybody has the germ of this type of revolt, things will
definitely change for the better. Because the condition of his country is
scandalous beyond description, Kassoumi is determined that, in spite of
Saif, his whole existence will continue to be a protest. His duty of
violence is to be a revolutionary, capable of resolving the contradictions
within himself and also within his society; he will reconcile his role of a
poet with that of a soldier, and use violence to achieve real political
freedom.

A semiotic interpretation of *Bound to Violence* will make us understand
fully the use made by Ouologuem of the theory and practice of violence in
its various forms. In this essay a few 'sordid happenings' have been

selected to highlight the continuing necessity of violence in view of the scandals that exist in both dependent and independent countries of Africa. Perhaps because the alternatives are few Ouologuem advocates the continued use of violence. It is time we saw the 'dawn' in the forest of darkness, that is, the history of Nakem as presented through the use of an epic form full of signs and symbols. As Saif says at the end of the book while playing one last game with Bishop Henry, 'Symbols never die'. We should go on interrogating a work of art until we get answers that enrich our actions, although we should not insist that any answer is final and all-embracing. As to the intractable and resilient nature of works of art when it comes to their interpretation, it seems apt to recall what an old Greek sage once said about the Lord of the Oracle: 'Oute Legei, oute Kryptei, alla semainei.' That is, He neither says, nor hides, he signifies. Ouologuem's language in *Bound to Violence* signifies a lot.

References

1. First published under the title *Le Devoir de Violence* (Paris, Editions du Seuil, 1968). Further references are to *Bound to Violence* (London: Secker & Warburg, 1971), and will be inserted in the essay.
2. R. Barthes, 'Elements of semiology', *Communication*, 4 (1964), p. 92. Author's translation.
3. E. Buyssens, *La Communication et l'articulation linguistique* (Brussels and Paris, 1967), p. 13. Author's translation.
4. L. Prieto, *Seminologie* (Paris, 1967), p. 95. Translation mine.
5. Buyssens, op. cit.
6. *West Africa*, 14 December 1968, p. 1474.
7. Abiola Irele, 'A new mood in the African novel', *West Africa*, 20 September 1969, pp. 113–15.
8. Mbelolo ya Mpiku, 'From one mystification to another: Negritude and Negraille in *Le Devoir de Violence*', *Review of National Literatures*, II, 2 (Fall 1971), p. 142.
9. Eric Sellin, 'The unknown voice of Yambo Ouologuem', *Yale French Studies*, 53 (1976), pp. 137–62.
10. André Schwartz-Bart, in a letter dated 16 August 1968 to Editions du Seuil.

8
Tradition and Social Criticism in Ahmadu Kourouma's *Les Soleils des indépendances*

▼▼▼▼▼▼▼▼▼▼▼▼▼▼▼▼▼▼▼▼▼▼▼▼▼▼▼▼▼

KWABENA BRITWUM

SENEGAL and the Cameroons seem to have produced a dispropor-tionately large number of the outstanding writers from French-speaking West Africa. For a long time, the Ivory Coast was rep-resented mainly by Bernard Dadié, incidentally one of Africa's most prolific and versatile writers, although there were lesser figures like Ake Loba, author of the well-known novel, *Kocoumba, l'étudiant noir* (1960), and the talented dramatist Charles Nokan. The situation changed in 1968 with the publication of *Les Soleils des indépendances*,[1] undoubtedly one of the finest novels ever written by an African. At once, its author, Ahmadou Kourouma, emerged as one of Africa's outstanding novelists.

Les Soleils is a remarkable novel. Rich and dense, it calls for all the resourcefulness at the critic's disposal. Its formal features and, in par-ticular, its language are very original and deserve serious study. How-ever, this essay will concentrate on what is perhaps a more urgent task, to throw light on the novel's meaning, by exploring some of the areas where its fictional world relates to its outer social reference.

Even a cursory reading of *Les Soleils* would identify the society in the text as distinctly Malinke. Thus the novel may be said to be about the Malinkes. But, like every novel, it mediates that referential society through the obliquities of language and narrative. While the social reality that appears in the novel is most meaningful when related to the Malinke society outside the text, this verbalized society is both the result of representing and a way of seeing the outer social world. Ahmadou Kourouma is himself a Malinke, steeped in the traditions of his people. But he is also a well-educated Ivoirian with a modernist outlook; he is an actuary by profession. Kourouma chooses to express his observations about his people through a created self (often the narrator), or sometimes more subtly through a fictional character like Fama. He maintains a critical distance between his people and himself, by adopting a satirical tone.

It is especially through the delineation of Malinke ontological and religious beliefs that we recognize Malinke society in the novel. For example, when Fama Doumbouya has a bad dream, he goes to see Balla, the fetish priest, who explains that it is because Fama's *dja* or 'spiritual self' has left his body, having been chased out by witches who feed on people's *dja*. Among the Malinkes, the narrator explains, each person has a 'guardian spirit' and it is responsible for terminating a man's earthly existence. This particular ontological belief has parallels among other African peoples: the Ewe *se*, the Igbo *chi* or the Akan *okra*, for example. The Malinkes hold other beliefs which similarly find echoes elsewhere in Africa. Kourouma often refers to these beliefs with a touch of irony. When, on a misty harmattan morning, the sun is hardly visible, the narrator describes the weather in the way that a traditional Malinke would see it: 'for a long time the harassed sun has to find its way through a tangle of mist, smoke and clouds' (p. 125). But the explanation for the state of the weather at that particular time is that Balla's fetish is angry. It is only after it has been pacified in the appropriate manner that the sun is allowed to appear, later the same day. The narrator does not attribute these beliefs only to those characters who reveal them but shows that these are traditional beliefs held by the Malinkes as a whole.

Malinke religious beliefs are not very different from those of some other African peoples. Like the Hausas in northern Nigeria, the Malinkes are essentially Muslim, and the Islamic religion can be said to be a part of their tradition – which is why they refer to their non-Islamized, Malinke-speaking kinsmen as 'Bambaras'.[2] Part of Kourouma's objective in this novel is to scrutinize Malinke-Islamic identity. For example, when Fama recovers from his nightmarish experience, his first reaction as a true Muslim is 'to recite scrupulously chapters of the Koran known to drive away evil spirits' (p. 123). However, when he goes, the following morning, to consult Balla, the great fetish priest at Togobala, he is acting contrary to the precepts of his Islamic faith. Throughout the novel we find that the Malinkes subscribe to two apparently contradictory sets of beliefs; they seem torn between their apparent acceptance of Islamic faith and their strong attachment to indigenous, pre-Islamic beliefs.

There are two main ways in which Kourouma brings out these contradictions in his people. First, the narrator simply dramatizes, with hardly any comment, these conflicting beliefs. Thus, at a funeral all those present pray to both Allah and the spirits of their ancestors. In this way, they infringe the most important Koranic injunction, the acceptance of the uniqueness of Allah. Secondly, Kourouma emphasizes, through authorial interventions, the Malinkes' inherent contradictions and thus throws into relief the implicitly ironic posture that the narrator tends to adopt towards the Malinkes. He speaks, for instance, of their '*fausseté malinké*':

> The Malinkes have a contradictory character because what goes on within their minds is darker than their skins and what they say is whiter than their teeth. Are they animists or Muslims? The Muslim listens to the Koran and the pagan follows Koma; but at Togobala, everybody openly claims to be a Muslim and breathes as a Muslim, but in private they all fear the fetish. (p. 108)

That paradox at the heart of Malinke religious outlook also throws light on the syncretic nature of Islam as practised by the Malinkes. Or, put differently, it points to a somewhat uneasy coexistence of two conflicting elements in Malinke culture and make-up: 'neither a lizard nor a swallow' (p. 108), as the narrator revealingly describes the people.

In *Les Soleils* Kourouma appears to see the Malinkes' practice of Islam as superficial in this sense. Balla's overwhelming influence among the Malinkes does not merely symbolize their attachment to indigenous, pre-Islamic beliefs, but also the bastardization of the role of a marabout, represented in the novel by Abdoulaye who is appropriately described as a 'marabout-sorcier'. The narrator is clearly echoing the Malinkes' feelings towards the marabout when he remarks that the marabout has the reputation of being able 'to penetrate deep into the Invisible as if he was entering his mother's hut and could speak to spirits as if he were talking to pals. Were he to point his finger at a silk-cotton tree the trunk and its branches would die' (p. 66). Here Kourouma insinuates that the marabout as a holy man, or sometimes a diviner and medicine man who uses orthodox Islamic methods, has virtually been transformed by the Malinkes into an indigenous witch-doctor. Thus, *Les Soleils* portrays the Malinkes as a people who have not really Islamized their culture, but have indigenized Islamic religion. Throughout the novel, Kourouma appears to be deriding the Malinkes' adulteration of Islamic beliefs.

A recurring feature of the Malinkes' religious practice in *Les Soleils* is their general love of divination. They do not simply consult the Koran or the marabout; in fact, although they claim to be Muslims, they prefer going to the fetish 'Koma' which, they believe, predicts farther into the future than the Koran. The Malinkes' habit of seeking advice from their oracles is inseparable from their belief in omens. In this regard, it is revealing that the most important happenings in the novel are always preceded by some visible signs or omens; for the Malinkes the future is always embedded in some visible form in the present. Sometimes signs of an impending calamity may lead a Malinke to consult his fetish with the view to finding the right propitiatory rites with which to divert that calamity. Alternately, by sounding his oracle, an individual may be advised against certain contemplated actions which could bring misfortune. But not all calamities can be forestalled in this way.

In the novel, there are two main types of predictions or omens. First, there are omens of possible disaster which, provided the right action is taken in time, may not necessarily bring calamity. A case in point is the timely appeasement of the gods when a whirlwind at a funeral feast warns those present that their 'spirits' are angry. Secondly, there are prophecies or omens of inevitable calamity. Here, at best, by appropriate pacificatory rites the impending disaster might be mitigated somewhat. However, the important thing is that, either way, nothing unusual happens without the gods forewarning men. Moreover, if the individual is lucky, he may in some cases (provided, of course, that he pays heed to an oracle's prescription), even escape from a pre-ordained misfortune. For example, during each harmattan, the fetish, Koma, dances at the public square to 'reveal' the future and recommend the sacrifices to be made. The aim here is to divert future calamities. Such a conception of misfortune posits, at least, a partially optimistic view of fate. The famous anthropologist Herskovits has remarked that among Dahomeans although 'what is in store for a man is foredained', yet, through appropriate action, a misfortune can be averted: 'man lives secure in the conviction that between the inexorable fate laid down for an individual and the execution of that fate lies the possibility of the way out . . .'[3]

The narrator's ironic tone suggests that Kourouma probably does not believe literally in these oracular pronouncements and omens. Yet, throughout the novel, great events are always foreshadowed; which is another way of saying that omens and predictions are always proved right in the long run. In a sense, *Les Soleils* can be described as a novel of prophecy. Indeed, structurally, it is largely a series of successfully predicted prophecies. Thus, a typical narrative unit in the novel roughly conforms to the following pattern: Oracle – Prophecy – Omens – Fulfilment of Prediction. It is revealing that one of the novel's axes is the materialization, at the end of the novel, of the ancient prophecy concerning the eventual demise of the Doumbouya dynasty. In spite of the fact that the narrator tends to show a certain critical detachment from Malinke beliefs, Kourouma undoubtedly has a deep affection for

Malinke culture. In a sense, the novel is a dramatization of the beauty and resilience of traditional Malinke culture. In addition, as a critic of the post-independence set-up in Africa, Kourouma finds in these beliefs and practices both a kernel of wisdom and a way of driving home his message. The story of the last phase of Fama's life is replete with lessons. When Fama Doumbouya consults Balla's fetish about his journey back to the capital, he is told that it is inauspicious. As readers, we know the fate that lies in store for Fama if he overlooks Balla's warning. Therefore when the narrator, in line with Balla's prophetic advice, remarks aphoristically, 'A certain foolhardiness leads us to our doom' (p. 151), he is in fact seeing Fama's final tragedy from the traditional Malinke viewpoint. Similarly, when the narrator concludes Part II of the novel with the words, 'In fact, Fama's journey is indeed a fateful one' (p. 153), he is indirectly inviting the reader to see Part III as a logical demonstration of Balla's warning to Fama. There is thus an inevitability about Fama's death at the end, resulting from his persistent refusal to heed Balla's prophecy. The narrator constantly hints at Fama's failure to read the omens of his impending troubles with the Ebony Coast regime. And once the omens are not heeded, they are naturally followed by Fama's own ordeal: 'Fama didn't want to take note of the clap of thunder, he accordingly had to face the real storm and thunderbolt' (p. 164).

Fama's failure to heed the warning signals of imminent danger is an allegory of what will befall the rulers of the Ebony Coast if they fail to heed the omens of future political upheavals. Thus, Kourouma expects the reader to draw implicit parallels between the omens of Fama's approaching fate and the signs of political unrest in the Ebony Coast. Moreover, in the same way that oracular pronouncements and omens of disasters are always proved right in the novel, Kourouma insinuates that future political upheavals in the Ebony Coast are inevitable precisely because, unlike traditional Africans, 'the Republics of Independent Africa haven't set up institutions like the fetish or oracles to deal with disasters' (p. 160). Fama's dream of a holocaust that will engulf the entire capital of the Ebony Coast adds allegorical force to Kourouma's intimation of a future calamity which will befall the country if it fails to learn from the traditional African practice of divination.

Although one can sometimes detect the author's voice, on the whole the novel's central ideas are conveyed through its fictional characters who tend to act as the author's surrogates. The most important of them is clearly Fama. Yet it is difficult to establish a straightforward correlation between the author's own views and Fama's. True, the latter embodies the authorial criticism of certain socio-political realities, but his point of view often appears suspect and sometimes even unreliable. The point is that Fama is critical of the contemporary era partly because he has an axe to grind; he attributes his present straitened circumstances to the advent of independence. But the novel makes it clear that Fama was not doing very well as a *dioula* (Muslim trader) even before independence. He overstates the case when he attributes his present circumstances as an impoverished, jobless husband to the independence era, 'les soleils des indépendances'. The adverse effect of independence on traditional craftsmen and traders has been used by Camara Laye in *Dramouss* and Mongo Beti in *Perpétue* to attack some contemporary African regimes. Given Kourouma's compassion for the underdog, apparent throughout the novel, one may assume that he automatically endorses Fama's grievance against the post-independence regime. However, the narrator's ironic tone enables the reader to see Fama in a slightly different light; his sense of humiliation as an impoverished *dioula* does not inspire too much sympathy, because his interpretation of the cause of his predicament is not really shared by the narrator, who chooses instead to view Fama here with a certain detachment. We see more clearly this ironic distance between the author and his protagonist when, after independence, Fama reveals his ambitions. In spite of the fact that he is illiterate, he aspires to become either a general secretary of a sub-section of the party in power or the director of a co-operative society. Kourouma may sympathize with Fama's plight, but it is quite clear that the latter's unrealistic aspirations attract the author's irony. As the narrator wryly puts it: 'Fama remained an illiterate just as the donkey's tail remains unchanged' (p. 23).

The main reason for Fama's dissatisfaction with the post-independence period is that he ascribes the inevitable demise of the Doumbouya dynasty, of which he is the last prince, to the political situation ushered in by independence. But, historically, this is not entirely correct. The erosion of the power of the traditional rulers actually started during the colonial era, a fact which is intimated more than once in the novel by the narrator. However, it is true that, even though post-independence regimes in Africa perhaps did not consciously set out to undermine the power of the traditional rulers, in practice, the institution of the one-party state, the importance of elected representatives and the power of local party functionaries all contributed to accelerate the decline of chieftaincy in French West Africa in particular.[4] The narrator of *Les Soleils* clearly shows that he is aware of all this. Fama sees the one-party system as the principal cause not just of the decline of the Doumbouya dynasty, but also of most of the evils of the post-independence world. Kourouma, however, does not share Fama's sim-

plistic views, in spite of his imaginative sympathy for the last scion of the
Doumbouya dynasty. The novel points out the tragic inevitability of the
Doumbouya demise and the frustrations of Fama the traditionalist in a
changed politico-socio-economic world. Throughout, the narrator tends
to refer to the Doumbouya past as well as Malinke traditions in a
nostalgic tone, although he also derides Fama's heroic pretensions, his
histrionic posturing as the proud descendant of a great dynasty. Indeed,
Fama does not merely attract authorial irony; he emerges in the novel as
above all a comic figure.

Kourouma's ambivalence towards his protagonist is shown by the
fact that in spite of the narrator's apparently humorous disengagement
from Fama, the latter is still the author's mouthpiece, since the novel's
political satire is seen principally from his point of view. In other
words, Kourouma complicates his satirical treatment of contemporary
Ebony Coast by seeing the post-independence era mainly from Fama's
jaundiced viewpoint. Fama's obvious dislike of the one-party form of
government is probably an indication of Kourouma's own aversion for
the system. Once, the narrator openly interpolates: 'the one-party (do
you know?) resembles witches' secret society; the great initiates devour
other people's children' (p. 23). The common denominator in both
Nikinai and the Ebony Coast, the two countries represented in the
novel, is their practice of the one-party form of government, which puts
them in line with most independent African regimes. In focusing on
both socialist Nikinai and capitalist Ebony Coast, Kourouma is not
primarily interested in their unmistakably pronounced ideological dif-
ferences, even if he does not overlook them altogether. It is the impact
of the one-party administration on traditional life and institutions in
Fama's Horodougou, an area which is conveniently astride of the two
countries, that seems to provide the main basis for comparison between
the two regimes. Whereas the party in the Ebony Coast is not described
in detail but is merely referred to throughout the novel, the activities of
the LDN (suggestive of RDA, *'Rassemblement Démocratique Africain'*,
the common political party in many parts of French colonial West
Africa), the party in Nikinai, are highlighted.

Here, as elsewhere, Kourouma has recourse to various surrogates. He
employs the fictive device of letting a number of passengers who happen
to be travelling in the same lorry tell one another about their experiences
in Nikinai. Thus, we are told that under the pretext that socialism
signifies 'the end of man's exploitation by man', the party has progres-
sively deprived Diakité's father of his possessions; the old man's violent
resistance to the socialist programme leads, in the end, to his summary

trial and execution. Another passenger, Konaté, a 'refugee from social-ism', informs us that the introduction of a new currency in independent Nikinai immediately ruined the traders. Konaté is a patriot, sympathetic towards the party's socialist ideals, but he finds it hard to accept, even temporarily, 'famine, shortages, forced labour, prison . . .' (p. 88). Indeed, it is in Nikinai that Fama first comes to realize the inevitable limitations imposed on the authority of traditional rulers by a one-party regime. But the novelist actually pays scant attention to either the socialist programme of the LDN or its shortcomings, although he allows some political refugees to voice their grievances. Kourouma does not appear to be seriously hostile to socialism. What is significant is the novel's implicit assumption that there is not much difference between the two countries as far as one-party administration is concerned. In focusing on Nikinai, the novelist is inviting the reader to supply the missing, or rather implicit, parallels with the one-party regime in the Ebony Coast.

Clearly, the novel's main focus is the capitalist Ebony Coast, although the novel is not more ideologically biased against capitalism than it is in favour of socialism. In highlighting the plight of Fama, an impoverished *dioula* living in a slum in the Ebony Coast's capital, Kourouma is not primarily interested in the class of northern *dioulas* living in the capital. It is revealing that Fama is no longer a prosperous *dioula*, but a jobless Malinke. True, he likes to think of himself as set apart by birth and profession from the beggars, the blind, the maimed who can hardly conceal their misery, but the novelist shows him as belonging very much to the pariahs of society. In fact, Fama's condition provides Kourouma with the opportunity to raise one of the central issues in the novel: what has independence really brought to the ordinary man? In a powerful authorial interpolation, Kourouma himself provides an answer:

> Nothing except a National Identity card and a membership card of the One Party. They are the crumbs left for the poor following the general distribution of the fruits of Independence. They have the dryness and hardness of bull meat. One can bite it with the canine teeth of a famished mastiff, but one can't get anything out of it; nothing to suck. It is like tendon, one can't chew it. (p. 23)

Fama is one of these pariahs who crowd the little slum markets in search of alms. The one thing that they are sure of getting in plentiful supply is 'lagoon water . . . rotten and salty as well as the sky, either dazzling with fierce sunshine or loaded with rains which fall on the jobless who have neither shelter nor beds'. They have nothing else to do except 'roam about, stink, pray and listen to the rumblings of their empty stomachs'

(p. 62). Nobody seems to care for them, certainly not the affluent corrupt élite 'who could afford to have cloths made out of bank notes' (p. 66). It is the novel's unrelenting focus on the lot of the 'wretched' which adds ideological substance to its criticism of the post-independence era.

Kourouma shows us the post-independence era from the standpoint of the underprivileged. He deliberately makes Fama yearn for the colonial era:

> Fama deeply regretted having fought and hated the French so much, a bit like the little plant which complained because the giant silk-cotton tree was absorbing all the sunshine. When the cotton tree was felled, the fragile plant directly received the fierce sun and the strong wind which killed it. (pp. 20–1)

The French colonial regime is seen as an impediment but also a bulwark against inclement elements. The narrator stresses that Fama hates colonialism and yet is not blind to the good things of the colonial period; for Fama the one positive side of the colonial administration is that it did not interfere with the 'business' of the *dioulas*. Kourouma hardly disguises his sympathy for Fama's viewpoint. He intimates that, for many an ordinary, impoverished African, faced with the hardships of the post-independence world, the colonial period has come to appear, however unjustly or wrongly, as an ideal era. It is left to the narrator to balance the picture, by saying that neither colonialism nor independence has done much good to the ordinary African. Kourouma's concern for 'the damned of the earth', to whom independence has brought practically nothing, links him with other African novelists such as Meja Mwangi, Sembene Ousmane, Ayi Kwei Armah and Mongo Beti. In *Les Soleils* Kourouma confers on this familiar theme a great poetic force.

The two countries in the novel, Nikinai and the Ebony Coast, are representative of independent Africa; their socio-political situation is, to a large extent, applicable to many independent African states. It does not really matter where one places the socialist state of Nikinai because it is less central to the novel's concerns. But it is crucial for the reader to know what the Ebony Coast really represents. Surprisingly, it is not a difficult task. Obviously, the name 'Ebony Coast' is meant as a parody of the Ivory Coast. In addition, there are several allusions intended to help the reader to identify the novel's historico-geographical point of reference, especially its principal setting, the Ebony Coast's capital. Both its topographical details and climate point out the capital in question as Abidjan. On the thorny question of alleged French dominance in the Ivory Coast, two historians have recently pointed out: 'Among educated Ivoirians there is much resentment at the slow pace of Africanization since Independence, which leaves French nationals a decade later still occupying jobs at the level of clerk and shop-assistant.'[5] This is undoubtedly an explosive issue in any discussion of the contemporary Ivory Coast. Kourouma therefore uses an apparently naive mouthpiece, Sery, the driver's apprentice, to make the point, and even he appears to be merely reporting other people's views:

> our students and intellectuals told us to drive away the French; that would have given us more houses, money and goods. But it was difficult, there were the French troops and also it wasn't good, because without the French there would be no work and we wouldn't like to be unemployed. (pp. 89–90)

When Sery observes 'All told, we toil and it is foreigners who get all the money' (p. 91), he is directly echoing the narrator's ideological stand: 'Buildings, bridges, roads over there [i.e. in the predominantly white area of the capital] were all built with black labour and yet they are occupied by, and belong to, whites. Independence can't change that . . .' (p. 18). For Kourouma, the French dominance in his country is one of the reprehensible features of the post-independence period. Thus, like a good deal of Africa's most recent writings, *Les Soleils* is based on the assumption that the advent of independence has not stopped 'neo-colonial' exploitation of the continent.

Les Soleils is a complex novel which calls for 'plural' readings, the kind of novel which frequently frustrates the critic's imperialistic attempts to domesticate or 'naturalize'[6] it with his reading strategy. However, from whatever angle one reads it, one cannot miss two of the novel's axes: its critical celebration of traditional African culture and its criticism of post-independence African politics. It is one of the most authentically African novels, and possesses a remarkably original perspective. Without being uncritical of tradition, *Les Soleils* views independent Africa mainly through the critical lens of a traditional African nurtured on the culture and worldview of his people. It speaks about Africans, not without affection, but without excessive indulgence. Above all, it speaks to Africans with an African voice.

References

1. *Les Soleils des indépendances* (henceforth referred to as *Les Soleils*), first published by Presses de l'université de Montréal (1968); reprinted by Editions du Seuil (Paris, 1970). Subsequent page references are to the du Seuil edition of the novel and will be inserted in the essay. All translations from the original French text are the author's own. An English translation is in preparation for inclusion in the African writers series.

2. Paul Marty, *Études sur l'Islam en Côte d'Ivoire* (Paris, 1922), p. 78.

3. Quoted by Meyer Fortes, 'The notion of fate in West Africa', in P. J. M. McEwan and R. B. Sutcliffe (eds.), *The Study of Africa* (London, Methuen, 1965), p. 77. See also Basil Davidson, *The Africans: An Entry to Cultural History* (London, Longman, 1969), pp. 139–40.

4. See Aristide R. Zolberg, *One-Party Government in the Ivory Coast* (Princeton, NJ, Princeton University Press, 1964).

5. Michael Crowder and Donal Cruise O'Brien, 'Ivory Coast: recent history', in *Africa South of the Sahara* (London, Europa Publications, 1971), p. 388. See also Samir Amin, 'Ivory Coast: economy', in ibid., pp. 389–91.

6. For an illuminating discussion of critics' practice of 'naturalization' of literary texts, see Jonathan Culler, *Structuralist Poetics, Structuralism, Linguistics and the Study of Literature* (London, Routledge & Kegan Paul, 1975), pp. 131–60.

9
Self and Other
in Sembene Ousmane's *Xala*

▼▼▼▼▼▼▼▼▼▼▼▼▼▼▼▼▼▼▼▼▼▼▼▼▼

FÍRINNE NÍ CHRÉACHÁIN-ADELUGBA

THE title of Sembene Ousmane's latest novel, *Xala*, translated from the Wolof, means 'impotence'. The central figure, El Hadji Abdou Kader Bèye, an enterprising middleman grown rich in independent (or neo-colonial) Senegal, has just married his third wife when the *xala* hits him, and the novel tells of his efforts to 'become a man again'. *Xala* was published thirteen years after the novel which is generally considered to be Ousmane's masterpiece, *God's Bits of Wood*. And, as one reads *Xala*, one cannot help being aware of certain echoes from the earlier work. For example, several of the characters in the earlier novel seem to reappear, older and wiser, in the later work. The central figure in *Xala*, El Hadji Abdou, had been a poor schoolmaster involved in trade union activities and fighting alongside the Bakayokos and the Lahbibs. His daughter, Rama, is the older counterpart of Bakayoko's adopted daughter Adjibid'ji, having 'grown up during the struggle for Independence . . . taken part in street battles and pasted up posters at night'.[1] His senior wife, Awa Astou, recalls Bakayoko's equally passive and docile Assitan. Naturally, too, certain themes recur. Ousmane's attitude to polygamy, religion and linguistic imperialism has not changed much in thirteen years.

However, it is these very echoes in *Xala* which bring home to us the distance which separates the respective worlds of the two novels. What has happened, for instance, to Banty Mam Yall, God's bits of wood, that huge lively throng of workers and their families, whose right to stage centre in the earlier work nobody dared dispute? Thirteen years later, they are no more to be seen. The classes in *Xala* have been polarized into the up-and-coming local middlemen, on the one hand, and on the other, the beggars. The workers' syndicate has been pushed aside to make room for the businessmen's group. The hovels of thirteen years ago have been taken off, the new set consisting of bourgeois villas bulging with imported furniture. The beggars, for their part, only take over the stage in the final scene. And, in contrast to the very human, multi-dimensional workers of *God's Bits of Wood*, what a bunch of grotesque monsters they are, deliberately dehumanized by Ousmane, perhaps to underline the extent to which they have been dehumanized by 'independent' Senegal. Above all, the common cause of the railway workers has, in *Xala*, become the private problem – very private! – of a single El Hadji. Naturally, the tone has also changed to match the change of cast and set: in *God's Bits of Wood*, almost every one of the many characters has some claim to our sympathy. In *Xala*, hardly a single character escapes ironic treatment.

But it is when we consider human relationships that the full impact of the evolution – of Senegal, or Ousmane, or both – from *God's Bits of Wood* to *Xala*, strikes us fully. In the earlier novel, the relationship of Self to Other was presented to us as one of complete interdependence. In this respect, the strike served Ousmane's purpose very well. Survival itself was impossible without the recognition of this interdependence: go it on your own and like, Sounkaré the blackleg, you get eaten alive by rats. But it is not hard times alone which make for the constant interplay between Self and Other which we find on every page of *God's Bits of Wood*: one's sense of Self, one's whole identity, is inseparable from the Other and the group. Separation is, quite simply, death. This is the meaning of the title, and it is made explicit in the little scene where Penda tries to count the unruly mob of women marchers. 'Ne nous dénombre pas',[2] begs one of them, 'We are God's bits of wood . . . you will make us die' (p. 266).

The world of *Xala* is very different. Self and Other have been dichotomized. As the title of *God's Bits of Wood* reflects the interdependence of Self and Other, so the new title, *Impotence*, expresses the impossibility of any real contact between Self and Other. Ousmane himself has hinted at what has happened in the interval. In 1964, in *L'Harmattan*, Leye the painter put Senegal's problems down to 'the chase after fridges, luxury cars and air-conditioners'.[3] And in an interview in 1969, Ousmane declared that since independence in Senegal, 'Money is the only apparent value left'.[4] The fight for children's allowances, the railway workers' main grievance in *God's Bits of Wood*, was obviously a group affair, but in the chase after fridges, cars and air-conditioners, it is every man for himself. We are in the world of independent enterprise, as we see in a very literal way right from the first pages of *Xala*, in the brief history of El Hadji Abdou's business career. Dismissed from teaching for trade union activities (in true *God's Bits of Wood* style), he had first gone into partnership, but by the time independence came he had dispensed even with his partner, and set up completely on his own: 'il fit cavalier seul' (p. 10).

The Self/Other dichotomy applies equally on the private as it does on the public level. It is significant that *Xala* opens with a meeting of the Chamber of Commerce, which is immediately followed by the wedding of El Hadji, a respected Chamber member, to his third wife. These two types of relationship – the commercial and the sexual, the public and the private – are inseparable throughout the novel. The plot itself reflects their inextricable nature: it is El Hadji's sexual bankruptcy which brings about his financial impotence. The world which provides the structures and vocabulary for relationships in *Xala* is that of commerce, where the Other is held at arm's length and seen as customer or seller or even as goods, where the Self–Other relationship is a matter of supply and demand, of gluts and shortages, profits and losses, of competitors, mergers, and the ever-present threat of bankruptcy. And Ousmane has chosen the sexual relationship as the major illustration of his theme, not because he wants to write pornography or even out of an interest in the problems of polygamy, but precisely because of the paradox involved: sex symbolizes, in the most graphic fashion, not the dichotomy of Self and Other, but their fusion in one flesh. What could be more ironic than sex to illustrate how, in the *Xala* world, the dispassionate commercial mentality dictates every thought, word and gesture?

The overflow of the businessman's mentality into private life is seen at its most fundamental in the relationship between El Hadji, the girl who will become his third wife, N'Goné, and her aunt, Yay Bineta. Yay Bineta plays the merchant or, more precisely, the middleman: for, just as El Hadji is a middleman in the commercial sense, she is his exact equivalent in the world of private relationships, not producing the goods (sex) herself, merely trading in them for profit. El Hadji's role is obviously that of customer, and N'Goné is the goods. In fact, as is often the case on the consumer market, El Hadji has no real need for N'Goné: she is a luxury item, since he already possesses two earlier but still functioning models. It is up to Yay Bineta, who needs a sale in order to survive – 'Look how we live, like animals in a yard' (p. 7) – to persuade him of the desirability of investment. This is how she introduces her niece, more or less offering her by the yard or the gallon: 'El Hadji, this is my daughter N'Goné. Take a good look at her. Could she not be a kind of measure? A measure of length or a measure of capacity' (p. 7). N'Goné herself has no say whatsoever in the whole transaction. She is an object from start to finish: for her aunt, she is a means to the latter's future security; for El Hadji, something of a white elephant, for he does not really need her, he has simply been won over by the clever display and the sales talk. Even the girl's mother sees her daughter in commercial terms: 'You don't keep a girl as if she was a gold coin. Even with a gold coin, you do business' (p. 104). And the narrative technique underscores N'Goné's role as a commodity: we see inside the minds of both buyer and seller, but we never find out what the goods thinks about it all.

Unfortunately, somewhere along the line the deal goes wrong. The goods are delivered on approval, but the customer must still sample and pay the balance. The car and the villa will never be N'Goné's if she turns out to be second-hand. El Hadji is encouraged by one and all: 'Va consommer ta vierge' (p. 42),[5] the traditional language of sex here lending itself admirably to the commercial world of *Xala*. But because of his malady, 'la consommation lui semblait impossible' (p. 65), the consumer is incapable of consuming, and the goods remain untouched and unapproved. We never find out whether N'Goné was new or second-hand. And El Hadji, since the effect of the sales-talk has had time to wear off during his illness, spends the rest of the novel wondering what to do with goods he has never really wanted, but, on account of the heavy investment, can only get rid of at a loss: 'It would not upset him to leave her . . . Yet to drop her after all he had spent . . . The car. And the villa. And all the other expenses . . .' (p. 29).

With characters like these, we have certainly come a long way from the idealistic love of *God's Bits of Wood* where N'Deye Touti could have married Beaugosse with his petit bourgeois pretensions and devoted her life with him to the chase after fridges and air-conditioners, but chose instead to break her heart over Bakayoko. In *L'Harmattan*, Tioumbé loves Sori in spite of his meagre means as bicycle-repairer. This is not to say that the earlier Ousmane was incapable of seeing 'love' in anything short of idealistic terms. He has always recognized that for many, the man–woman relationship is based on more pragmatic issues. As one of the characters in *White Genesis* put it: 'When a woman goes to bed with you, either she loves you or she has her eye on your harvest'.[6] The only difference is that in *Xala* the either/or has been virtually eliminated, and the harvest had better be a good one. If not, as Oumi N'Doye, El Hadji's second wife tells him, with a sound sense of the laws of supply and demand: 'I warn you, I can go elsewhere' (p. 66). And when he goes bankrupt, this is precisely what she does.

So, in *Xala*, the relationship between Self and Other can be seen as that of buyer, seller and goods, with sex the principal commodity. El Hadji's *xala* provides yet another example of how sex can be bought and sold. He has lost his 'manhood', but, as he sees it, getting it back is simply a matter of how much one is willing to pay: 'I want to be cured. Become a man again. Tell me how much you want' (p. 54). Of course, there is nothing new in the idea of paying for services rendered, medical or otherwise. What is somewhat new in *Xala* is the withdrawal of the cure by the doctor when the cheque bounces!

In this world, where money is all that matters in personal relation-ships, it is the beggar alone who, in the last few pages, reminds us that this is not the only way in which man can relate to man, and that, quite literally, 'becoming a man again' is not a matter of how much you can pay. He, too, offers to restore El Hadji's 'manhood', and even proposes the deal in the sort of language which is most meaningful to the El Hadjis of this world: 'I want my payment in advance' (p. 110); 'you can take it or leave it' (p. 113). But he uses this language ironically, for in fact, as he adds, 'I haven't asked for any money' (p. 113). In the last scene he reminds us that not money but the willingness to recognize the existence of the Other, and especially the underprivileged Other, as exemplified by himself and his fellow beggars, is what can ultimately make El Hadji Abdou 'become a man again'.

The beggar tells El Hadji, 'You can take it or leave it'. His casual attitude is in striking contrast to that of the other characters, who seem to be continually driven by a sense of panic: panic to possess the goods, or the humans one sees as goods, and once one has got hands on them, to keep them strictly to oneself. It is ironic that in *God's Bits of Wood*, where the basic essentials of existence – food and water – were virtually unob-tainable, relationships should be based on the code of 'Nobody gets to eat unless his neighbour eats too',[7] whereas in *Xala*, where every page seems to overflow with milk and honey, sharing is seen as a crime against the Self. When Mam Fatou says 'You must plough your own field' (p. 6), she means one's own field and nobody else's. In the vehicle which takes all El Hadji's chidren to school, the children of the respective wives insist on their 'own bench'. Far from sharing with one's neighbour, one is unwil-ling to share with even one's half-brothers. As Rama puts it, when the idea is proposed to offer shelter to Oumi's homeless children: 'This house belongs to our mother. It is out of the question to have our half-brothers and sisters here' (p. 103).

This panic-striken insistence on private property emanates from what we might call the 'middleman complex'. The pages of *Xala* may abound in long lists of luxury goods and descriptions of fine cars, fine clothes and

sumptuously furnished villas, but we should not think of these items as
the property of the characters any more than they do themselves. They
are, in fact, all painfully aware of their position as mere middlemen on
the line from producer to consumer. El Hadji owes his wealth to acting as
a front for neo-colonialist interests. Many goods pass through his hands,
but none of them is his. He is no more than a go-between, living largely
on credit. In this respect, his position is that of 'independent' Senegal in
miniature. As he himself says to his fellow-members of the businessmen's group, 'Who owns the banks? The insurance companies? The
factories? The businesses? The wholesale trade? The cinemas? The
bookshops? The hotels? All these and more besides are out of our
control' (p. 92). Later in the same speech he will refer to all the members
of the group as 'businessmen without funds'. El Hadji's words reveal the
two pet obsessions of the insecure middleman: ownership ('Who owns
the banks?') and control ('All these . . . are out of our control'). It is in
this light that we should interpret his angry reply to his daughter when
she dares to question his authority: 'You can be a revolutionary at the
university or in the street, but not in my house. Never!' (p. 13). But
unfortunately, as he later discovers, his reference to *chez moi*, his private
property, is, like everything else connected with his middleman
activities, 'without funds', that is, without foundation. For, once he can
no longer deliver the sexual goods to his wives, he literally has no home.
He is forced instead to stay at the hotel, where the manager's words of
welcome have a peculiarly ironic ring: 'Ici, c'est ta maison' (p. 96). It is
his house, that is, as long as he can pay for it.

As usual, hand in hand with the idea of private property in terms of
material possessions runs the idea of the Other as private property to be
possessed, usually through sex. The wives in the polygamous set-up are
painfully aware that they have no private emotional property; and El
Hadji, for his part, in typical middleman style, simply moves between
them, appearing to possess all three but in reality possessing none. But it
is in the poetic justice of the beggar's dealings with El Hadji that
Ousmane really shows how inextricably the two types of private property
– inanimate and human – are intertwined. The beggar, whom El Hadji
had dispossessed of his land, in turn prevents El Hadji, through the spell
which makes him impotent, from the 'possession' of his new wife.

Obsessed with the notion of private property, the Self in *Xala* persists
in shutting itself in, shutting the Other out, in closing its eyes to the
existence of the Other, especially the Other it has dispossessed, and trying
to convince itself that, within its own private castle, it is in control: 'You
can be a revolutionary . . . in the street, but not in my house.' Once

again, it is the beggar who cracks the illusion. El Hadji had tried to go even further with the beggar than he did with his daughter, by having the fellow banished from the street itself. But the street is public, not private, property; and the beggar returns, to cast his spell on the most private part of El Hadji's private property! This is one message the *xala* has for us: it is difficult to sustain the illusion that one has property and that one controls what happens to it when one has lost control of that one piece of property that one might legitimately call one's own! Another message is that one cannot shut oneself in and relegate the revolution to the street: sooner or later the beggar, followed by his horrific band of broken-down subhumanity, will invade one's house, one's fridge, one's bed, as they do El Hadji's in the final scene. It is in this last scene that Ousmane makes his final ironic dig at the whole concept of private property: the police who have been called to relieve El Hadji of his unwelcome guests politely withdraw, leaving him to his fate, with the words, 'We respect private property' (p. 113).

The panic to possess and the obsession for private property stem from the twin threats of the business world: shortage of supply on the one hand and poor markets on the other. In *Xala* the item in short supply is the man. As Yay Bineta puts it, 'There is a queue of girls waiting for husbands that stretches from here to Bamako' (p. 6). The answer is the severe rationing we find in polygamy – no more than three days each at a time, in strict rotation. So, as soon as one gets one's hands, literally, on one's share, is it any wonder that one should do as Oumi N'Doye does, 'le caresser gloutonnement'? (p. 65). In the woman's case sex is also a product to be sold, but here the converse applies: there is a glut on the market, a severe case of oversupply and underdemand. The result is an acute sense of competition, a determination to display one's goods to advantage. No one is more determined than Oumi N'Doye who, conscious of her disadvantageous position in the market (she is the middle wife and refers to herself bitterly as 'optional'), goes all out to put on an impressive display: 'Oumi N'Doye had prepared her *aye* in keenly competitive spirit . . . She wanted to make him forget the last meal he had had with his first wife . . . The planning of the meal was part of . . . the campaign to reconquer lost ground' (p. 55).[8]

The acute sense of competition acts naturally, in most cases, as a divisive force. In contrast to Mame Sofi and Bineta, the happily united 'rivales' of *God's Bits of Wood*, El Hadji's two wives, Awa Astou and Oumi N'Doye, acknowledge that they have seen each other only seven times in seventeen years. On the other hand, recourse to the merger as a means of combating the threat of a new competitor is as logical here as it is in the business world. Thus, for once, Astou and Oumi present a united front as they watch together the takeover of the market by the newcomer N'Goné. The merger replaces in *Xala* what in Ousmane's earlier works might simply be called friendship. The idea of friendship is almost completely absent in the later novel. If Awa Astou, one of the more sympathetic characters 'had no friends' (p. 45), this is even truer of all the others. In a context where the Other is seen as rival, where sharing is inconceivable, where one is perpetually suspicious of the Other, the kind of warm, reciprocal, give-and-take relationship between Dieynaba and Maimouna in *God's Bits of Wood*, between N'Goné War Thiandum and Gnagna Guissé in *White Genesis*, is hardly to be expected. El Hadji may appear to have a friend in the president of the Chamber of Commerce, whom he can at least talk to about his *xala*. But we should note the language in which Ousmane presents this friendship to us: 'When [the president] spoke of El Hadji's *xala*, he used a throaty voice with a sympathetic ring to it, which around here is always associated with the desire to be helpful' (p. 68).[9] The president's desire is not to be helpful, but simply to appear to be so. His manner with his 'friend' is as calculated as all moves in the business world. In *Xala*, one merges with the Other while he can be useful to the Self, and drops him as soon as his useful days are over. This is what El Hadji had done to his business partner, and what the president, in turn, will do to El Hadji.

In the language of the *Xala* world, the meaning of the word 'friend' has, not unnaturally, been stretched to embrace the new realities. Thus the seer warns El Hadji to watch out for 'a friend who wished him ill', neither El Hadji nor the seer apparently seeing any contradiction in the phrase.[10] Once again, only the beggar uses words as the characters in *God's Bits of Wood* might have used them. When he introduces himself to El Hadji in the final scene with the words, 'It is me, with my friends' (p. 109), the beggar is implying, in true *God's Bits of Wood* style, that the Self, the 'me', would not be complete without the Other. To him, friends are those who share a common lot with one, and with whom it would be unthinkable not to share whatever spoils, like the contents of El Hadji's fridge, come one's way.

The fact that the characters of *Xala* tend to see life predominantly in terms of business deals affects the Self–Other relationship not merely in how people think of each other, but in all forms of contact: the touch, the look, the way they talk to each other. El Hadji's *xala* is symbolic: it makes natural, spontaneous interaction impossible. All moves are calculated, and nothing is ever reciprocal. True, there are numerous instances of physical contact: Mariem's arms around her father's neck, El Hadji and his two wives rubbing elbows in the back of the Mercedes, Oumi's hands on El Hadji in bed. But what is the motivation? Mariem 'joyfully' embraces her father, and in the next breath asks him for money; Oumi crams into the back seat of the Mercedes to deprive Astou of the pleasure of riding alone with El Hadji; Oumi's hands on her husband's body 'caress him greedily', not from love or even desire, but from a determination to win back her property. What is missing in *Xala*, in terms of physical contact, is the kind of joyful acknowledgement of the Other which Bakayoko in *God's Bits of Wood* experiences when he arrives at the strikers' mass meeting: 'They recognized him . . . and held out their hands.'[11] The same phrase, 'to hold out one's hand' is used in *Xala* by N'Goné's mother, but when she refers to 'des gens qui peuvent nous tendre la main' (p. 16), we can be sure she means a hand with something more substantial than warm physical contact to offer.

Eye-contact between Self and Other follows a similar pattern. The kind of transparency which exists between Gnagna Guissé and N'Goné War Thiandum in *White Genesis*, where 'each looked into the other's eyes and saw herself reflected there'[12] would be unthinkable in the *Xala* world. More typical is the look which passes between Awa Astou and El Hadji Abdou: 'Her eyes . . . had a deep inscrutability that seemed like a total absence of reaction . . . El Hadji could not sustain her look. He turned away . . .' (p. 14). In a world of calculated manoeuvres, the last thing one wants is to meet someone's gaze, lest he read in your eyes the next move you intend to pull on him. Rather, in *Xala*, the mutual gaze is replaced by the look which seeks to master the Other at no cost to the Self. Thus Yay Bineta, unobserved herself, observes El Hadji in an attempt to assess the state of his sexual health, upon which her deal with him depends: 'She watched him, unobserved, as she spoke. Her widow's instinct . . . detected the smell of wrinkled skin emanating from the male sitting opposite her . . .' (p. 102). Here, not only the look but even the sense of smell is exploited in the attempt to grasp the Other, the better to manipulate him as customer or as goods. If the sort of spontaneous, reciprocal reaching out to the Other, so common in *God's Bits of Wood*, is absent in *Xala*, this other kind of close contact ironically abounds. Every intimate detail of El Hadji's existence is known to the entire neighbourhood, while he is paradoxically incapable of any intimacy at all with his new wife. His physical nakedness in the final scene is nothing in comparison with the way his acquaintances have stripped his inner soul naked from the moment his *xala* becomes known. The image for this type of intimate probing of the Other for one's own purposes is the termite, which 'eroded people from the inside, leaving only the outward form of its victims intact' (p. 156).[13] And the 'hollow men' which result from this kind of Self–Other contact are symbolized by the tailor's dummy which Yay Bineta thrusts into El Hadji's lap in place of N'Goné after the deal has finally been undone.

Finally, how does the mentality produced by the 'chase after fridges' manifest itself in terms of verbal communication between Self and Other? In *God's Bits of Wood*, although the stomachs of the characters may be empty, almost every conversation between them is a verbal feast. They communicate endlessly with each other about anything and everything, from the revolution to N'Deye Touti's new brassière. In *Xala*, once again, this spontaneity and reciprocity are missing. The 'conversation' between Oumi and El Hadji where she tries to recover her lost ground is fairly representative: she chatters on and on, but El Hadji hardly hears a word, preoccupied as he is with his own thoughts, and especially with suspicions that Oumi herself may well be the source of his *xala*.

In *Xala*, people not only talk less, they also talk less well. The characters of *God's Bits of Wood* have an apt comment for every situation. In *Xala*, as the narrator bluntly tells us, we should expect no more than 'banal chatter' and 'trite, empty conversation' (p. 63). This is understandable, considering that the type of talk for talk's sake, which in *God's Bits of Wood* makes up for so many material privations, profits no one in the chase after fridges. This is not, however, to imply that the characters in *Xala* are verbally inactive. They may not excel in 'conversations fines, délicates et spirituelles' (p. 98), but their use of verbal communication is in perfect harmony with the norms and values of the commercial world they inhabit.

In his earlier work, Ousmane has always emphasized the importance of verbal communication. The Word, besides being a means of lively everyday intercourse between Self and Other, is a weapon, and a weapon often more powerful than action itself. 'You have cut off the water, now come and cut off my tongue', yells Mame Sofi defiantly in *God's Bits of Wood*.[14] Indeed, it is the use of the Word as weapon in the service of the truth (and not sexual prowess, as El Hadji seems to think) which defines man: 'If a man loses the courage to proclaim the truth, he may as well die', says Dethye Law in *White Genesis*.[15] In *Xala*, there is only a single allusion to the power of the word as defined above. El Hadji's faithful driver, Modu, who comes from Wolof country 'where the spoken word is a red-hot iron' (p. 104), is one of the few characters who can still speak as they spoke in *God's Bits of Wood* and *White Genesis*. He applies the iron at its hottest, for instance, in his denunciation of Yay Bineta. Like the griot in *White Genesis*, Modu in this scene 'said what others dared not say'.[16] But Modu is an exception. The workers in *God's Bits of Wood*, like Dethye Law in *White Genesis*, aspired to an ideal world where 'no man dares to strike you because he knows you speak the truth'.[17] In *Xala*, Rama's slapped face bears witness to El Hadji's non-allegiance to such notions.

In the earlier novels, then, Word was weapon and Word and Truth were identical. In the commercial world of *Xala*, the Word is still some sort of weapon, or at least instrument: it is only the equation of Word to Truth that has been modified. Once again, we are hardly surprised: for surely a salient feature of commercial language is precisely the lack of any necessary one-to-one correspondence between Word and Truth, between publicity and product. Here, the relationship established by language is simply the one which best suits the salesman's interests, and the efficacy of language, as weapon or instrument, lies not in its ability to reflect truth, reality, or the actual quality of the goods, but to suspend the consumer's judgement. The Word of the earlier novels has become, in *Xala*, simply sales talk, or its social equivalent, 'playing to the gallery' (p. 18). In all types of Self–Other encounter, whether the scene by the Chamber of Commerce or Oumi N'Doye's bed, language, instead of reflecting reality, more often than not runs counter to it. Nowhere is the gap between what people say to the gallery or the consumer and what they really mean more obvious than at the second meeting of the Chamber of Commerce, where the decision is taken to banish El Hadji from their ranks. Publicly, they justify his exclusion in the name of 'morality', 'honesty' and 'the welfare of the people' (p. 92). In reality they mean that, because of El Hadji's misdeeds, 'none of us has been able to obtain credit for weeks' (p. 91). Admittedly, at this point El Hadji denounces neo-colonialist interests in a very fine speech worthy of Bakayoko himself. It is only the inspiration which is different. Where Bakayoko used the Word as weapon to improve the lot of millions, El Hadji uses it as a final desperate smokescreen to protect his own skin. The effect on the audience is also different: far from being carried away on a wave of revolutionary enthusiasm, the members of the Chamber of Commerce, businessmen like El Hadji, hence native speakers of *Xala* language, have no difficulty in interpreting his message: 'You're up to your neck in muck and you preach revolution to us. You should have thought of all that before' (p. 93). The Word is indeed impotent here, in the mouth of one who 'eats from the same dung-heap' (p. 92) as everyone else.

So interdependence and solidarity are no more. In 1960, Ousmane could write of workers who got together across half of Africa, who fought and won. In 1973, El Hadji has set up on his own, impotence has set in, and his salvation lies in the hands of a beggar. The message of *Xala* is very clear. *God's Bits of Wood*, for all its historical setting, surely shows us men and their inter-relationships, not as they are, or ever have been, but as they could be. It is a prescription for independence. *Xala*, on the contrary, is proscriptive. It is a lesson in how not to live, a cautionary tale warning all the El Hadji's of 'independent' Africa of the impotence which will inevitably befall them if they persist in their two inter-related follies: in being 'businessmen without funds' and in ignoring the existence of the beggars they themselves have created.

The cause-and-effect relationship which Ousmane establishes between El Hadji's refusal to acknowledge the beggar whom he has dispossessed, and his resulting impotence, may strike us at first glance as mere wishful thinking on the author's part: would that beggars could cast magic spells and render their oppressors impotent. But, in fact, Ousmane's feet are as firmly on the ground as ever. For what else is the beggar but the potential worker, the potential labour force which alone could make production possible, and without which El Hadji will always be a 'businessman without funds' and Senegal will always be impotent? *Xala*, then, is a plea to El Hadji to join forces with God's bits of wood before it is too late, so that together they may chase the neo-colonialist out of the market.

References
1. Sembene Ousmane, *Xala*, translated from the French by Clive Wake (London, Heinemann, 1976), p. 12. Quotations in English will be from this translation, except where otherwise stated. Page numbers will henceforth be inserted in the essay. Quotations in French will be from *Xala* (Paris, Présence Africaine, 1973), with page numbers inserted in the essay.
2. Sembene Ousmane, *Les Bouts de bois de Dieu* (Paris, Le Livre Contemporain, 1960), p. 290. Unless otherwise stated, quotations will be from *God's Bits of Wood*, trans. Francis Price (London, Heinemann, 1973). The translation 'Don't count us' does not give the same idea of breaking up an integrated whole.
3. Sembene Ousmane, *L'Harmattan* (Paris, Présence Africaine, 1964), p. 210. The translation is the author's, as to my knowledge a translation of this novel has not yet been published.
4. 'L'argent est devenu la seule valeur morale reconnue', *Bingo*, 195 (April 1969).
5. The effect is lost in Wake's translation: 'Off to deflower your virgin!' (p. 260).
6. Sembene Ousmane, *'Le Mandat' précédé de 'Véhi Ciosane'* (Paris, Présence Africaine, 1965), p. 80. The translation in this case is the author's. Quotations in English will henceforth, except where otherwise stated, be taken from *The Money Order* with *White Genesis*, trans. Clive Wake (London, Heinemann, 1972).
7. *Les Bouts de bois de Dieu*, p. 232. Author's translation.

8. Apart from the first sentence, the translation here is from Wake, op. cit.
9. Author's translation.
10. The same cannot be said for Clive Wake, who clearly had difficulty in stomaching such a contradiction, and ended up translating *'ami'* as 'colleague' (p. 43).
11. *Les Bouts de bois de Dieu*, p. 237. Author's translation.
12. *The Money Order* with *White Genesis*, p. 22.
13. Author's translation.
14. *Les Bouts de bois de Dieu*, p. 176. Author's translation.
15. *The Money Order* with *White Genesis*, p. 66.
16. ibid., p. 33.
17. *God's Bits of Wood*, p. 323.

10
Towards an Africanization of the Novel: Francis Bebey's Narrative Technique

▼▼▼▼▼▼▼▼▼▼▼▼▼▼▼▼▼▼▼▼▼▼▼▼▼▼▼▼▼▼

NORMAN STOKLE

A WESTERN reader, scrutinizing the novels of Francis Bebey, may be struck by their apparent lack of narrative consistency. It is as if the author had set out quite systematically to flout all the rules handed down by Flaubert, Henry James and Ford Maddox Ford. Objective narration and its attendant qualities of neutrality, impartiality and *impassibilité* are thrown to the winds as Bebey's narrators become either his direct spokesmen or enjoy a bonanza of self-indulgence, interpreting the facts, pronouncing judgements, offering advice and digressing at length on a host of subjects ranging from the trivial to the intellectually abstract. Far from adhering to the convention which requires that a story be told from one point of view, these same narrators adopt any stance convenient to their immediate purposes – omniscient author, author-participant, author-observer – within the confines of the same novel. In short, a dominant characteristic of Bebey's work is its polytonality.

Although familiar with Western novelistic techniques, having studied literature at two French *lycées* (La Rochelle and Louis le Grand) and at the Sorbonne, Bebey chooses quite consciously to discount them in favour of a more instinctive approach. As he puts it:

> I've never investigated the way I tell my stories very thoroughly. You know what I do? I just go ahead and write them. I've never once told myself that such-and-such a thing must be done in such-and-such a way.[1]

This insouciance produces a form of expression closely allied to that of the oral folktale as delivered by the traditional Doualan *conteur*. An examination of his three novels – *Le Fils d'Agatha Moudio* (1967), *La*

Poupée ashanti (1973) and *Le Roi Albert d'Effidi* (1976) – will demonstrate the point and highlight certain defects in Bebey's artistry.

Le Fils d'Agatha Moudio[2] may be viewed as the unhappy tale of a simple, good-hearted young fisherman, Mbenda, who is constantly victimized by the social system and the mischievous appetites of those around him. He ends up saddled with two wives, both of whom have been unfaithful to him and may well continue to be so, and two children, neither of whom is his. To crown all, he seems perfectly resigned to his fate. A similar sense of tragedy hangs over *La Poupée ashanti*,[3] set against the urban backdrop of Nkrumah's Accra. It is the drama of an attractive, intelligent and courageous girl who is seduced in primary school, denied an education, almost killed in a street demonstration, constantly badgered by her domineering grandmother, ultimately brainwashed into spending the rest of her life as a market vendor, and married to a husband whose values and educational level are so markedly different from her own that their future connubial happiness must be regarded at best as uncertain. Bebey's most recent novel, *Le Roi Albert d'Effidi*,[4] brings us the bitter-sweet tale of a successful middle-aged businessman who is almost destroyed by his political and marital ambitions. Albert's new and dangerously young wife, Nani, is unfaithful to him. He loses an election after a particularly turbulent campaign involving the virtual destruction of his car and his self-respect. Finally, his wayward wife returns to him, and Albert, setting aside his political ambitions and some of his long-held beliefs, returns to his neglected shop.

In their sense of tragedy, these novels are worthy of Balzac. Yet Bebey, for all his cynicism, is basically an optimist in regard both to Africa and to humanity in general. And, equally important, he has a wry sense of humour. He could no more make tragedies out of his stories than could Molière out of *Le Tartuffe*. To have done so would have been to sacrifice their delightful irony, their lightness of tone, their earthiness and ring of truth. It would also have been to violate Bebey's own nature. Such considerations help explain his choice of narrative stance.

In *Le Fils d'Agatha Moudio*, we see events and people through the eyes of Mbenda, the semi-literate fisherman himself. His view of reality is filtered quite predictably through his hopes and fears, prejudices, ignorance and acceptance of the cultural norms of traditional African life. No rebel or rugged individualist, Mbenda is an accurate reflector of the more general village point of view, the image of rural Africa. His principles are the standard ones: anti-corruption, anti-colonialist, respect for local heroes and village elders, and recognition of the need for hard work and honesty in human relationships. Since Mbenda is uncomplicated and fundamentally decent, and since his only desire is to live a quiet life in accord with the prevailing social mores, his narrative is spontaneous, direct, even intimate. We are ready to accept the sincerity of his word because he lacks the deviousness to tell us deliberate lies. Moreover, since it is clear from the closing pages of the novel that Mbenda is recounting the incidents of his story a number of years after they actually occurred, his narration must benefit in some way from the objectivity which comes with distance. In this sense, he is a reliable narrator. On the other hand, his chronic emotional problem – torn as he is between his tyrannical mother and an African version of Manon Lescaut – coupled with his ability to recall that problem with all the intensity of the present moment prevents him from achieving complete impartiality. Yet at the same time, this very intensity and immediacy enhance his narrative power. He knows how to captivate his audience, excite its curiosity and juggle with its emotions by withholding vital information or raising tantalizing questions while omitting to supply the answers. 'You'll know about that later. Listen to me now', he frequently declares as if in response to our questions. Elsewhere, he appeals for our attention: 'listen to the rest of my story'; or for our patience: 'you'll find that out presently'; or whets our appetite: 'that's another story; we'll come back to it later'. Such statements affirm the dynamic relationship between audience and narrator as well as the latter's tight control over the story.

Mbenda's narratory obtrusiveness, reminiscent of certain Augustan and Victorian novels, also takes the form of judgement, justification or condemnation of a character's behaviour, correction of a false impression, recollection of earlier incidents or statements which are subsequently proved correct, and his personal reactions – shock, disgust, perplexity, delight – to the unfolding action. He is also prone to self-approbation and to dispensing advice, particularly in the area of his greatest incompetence: marital relations. 'When two wives have something to say to each other', he counsels us, 'let them do so freely, even if you happen to be their common husband. Such insignificant things can assume great importance.' And in a similar vein, he confides to the aspiring polygamist: 'The universal tactic of polygamy resides in a carefully sustained discord between the wives.' These multiple judgements, justifications and demonstrations of grassroots wisdom betray his thorough-going social conformism and amuse the reader who, by definition, must be more educated, and therefore, perhaps, more enlightened, than Mbenda himself. The difference in educational level – a difference of which the narrator himself is oblivious – allows an ironic relationship to develop between the author and his narrative agent.

This particular technique, however, remains surprisingly under-exploited in *Le Fils d'Agatha Moudio*.

The shift to third-person narrators in *La Poupée ashanti* and *Le Roi Albert d'Effidi* is dictated by two considerations: the larger canvas of these novels and Bebey's desire for greater freedom to express his own views as an enlightened African. In *La Poupée ashanti*, we follow the activities and evolving attitudes of Edna and Mam, both illiterate vendors in the Accra Market; of Spio, the educated functionary in his widely shifting locations, of Gin and Angela and Aunt Princess in their personal lives; as well as the deliberations of bureaucrats and a government commission. Such manoeuvres lie beyond the scope of a first-person narrator, no matter how nimble. *Le Roi Albert d'Effidi* is more tightly focused, both geographically and socially. But here again, the struggle between the younger and older generations on the general level or between Albert and Bikounou on the personal level is too intense and too multi-faceted to be narrated with anything approaching completeness or objective balance by a single subjective agent. Even so, the striking feature of both novels is the close resemblance of their narrators to that of *Le Fils d'Agatha Moudio*. It is as though the issue of third- or first-person narrative stance were of small consequence, as though, magically, all narrators were blessed with identical powers irrespective of their angle of vision. There is that same playfulness with the reader ('Oh, you'll never guess'); the same relish for gossip and scandal (Edna's bastard origins, Aunt Princess's many lovers, Nani's almost certain infidelity); the same need to justify or condemn a character's behaviour (Spio's non-appearance at the demonstration, Mam's scolding of Edna, Father Bonsot's inappropriate sermon); the same impulse to interpret the facts as well as relate them (the significance of Spio's letter to Edna, the reason for Belobo's abrupt change of subject when talking to Albert); the same liberality with useful and useless advice (handle market women with care, mistrust certain public scribes, check early to make sure your wife's baby is yours). Again, we are reminded of previous incidents or statements bearing directly on the present action. Not only are we told how characters think and feel as the narrator trips freely from one to the other; we are also informed how they would have thought and felt in certain hypothetical circumstances. Their third-person stance notwithstanding, these narrators establish themselves as characters in their own right, with commanding personalities and a confidence in their own opinions bordering at times on cockiness.

In *La Poupée ashanti*, the narrator's intimate knowledge of sales techniques, beauty products, the Accra Market community and his attitude towards potential clients all point to his being a longstanding frequenter or even full member of that community himself. In no sense an impartial, impersonal narrator, he functions rather as a periodically omniscient observer with Market connections and decidedly Market sympathies. Although quite unashamedly a male chauvinist, he admires the Market women for their sense of solidarity, political influence and community spirit. His own nature even mirrors some of their shortcomings, not the least of these being his constant urge to digress or to proffer a personal opinion as the fancy takes him. Such fits of loquacity can be thoroughly entertaining, especially when they involve smutty rumours such as Aunt Princess's licentious life 'outside the walls', or the misadventures of her Hercules bicycle. At other times they are heavy with political implications, as when we are treated to a detailed examination of Nkrumah's statue in front of the Parliament buildings. Its inscriptions, full of righteous intentions, afford an eloquent contrast to the mediocre attitude of the politicians involved in the Amiofi affair. Similar digressions for the purpose of either humour, social commentary or both, occur in the other novels. Chapter 13 of *Le Roi Albert d'Effidi* is entirely devoted to a diagnosis of laughter and to the narrator's highly amusing explanation of how he would retail that commodity were he a trader. These various digressions, though appended to the central story by the most tenuous of threads, constitute refreshing pauses in the ongoing action.

Like his predecessors, the narrator of *Le Roi Albert d'Effidi* belongs to the society he is portraying ('Remember the day the men of Village-des-Palmiers . . .' or again, 'You know that avenue . . .'). But, unlike them, he seems more sophisticated and possesses a wider cultural and intellectual frame of reference.[5] This does not mean his narration is impartial. His sympathies are too heavily on Albert's side for that. It means simply that his opinions, judgements and descriptions are couched in a more extensive vocabulary which occasionally reaches poetic heights. Note his description of the music and dance spectacle in honour of Father Bonsot. Moreover, the range of topics for discussion and digression can legitimately be wider and their domain more abstract. We recall, here, his observations on African authenticity and his wry comments concerning the political situation in Africa as it prepares for 'the independence of its peoples and the consolidation of its under-development'.

By the yardstick of D. H. Lawrence or the objectivist-realist school of Flaubert and Maupassant, the unrestrained, self-assertive high jinks of Bebey's narrators are unforgivably immoral. But Bebey cares little for Occidental sacred cows, and even less for Occidental critics. His interests lie elsewhere; and so does his audience. Only by understanding the nature of that audience can we hope to uncover the underlying forces dictating his narrative approach.

Bebey's sustained association with Les Editions CLE in Yaoundé rather than with a French publisher indicates his deliberate, and logical, orientation towards the francophone African literate public.[6] His appeal is unequivocably to the African mind, a mind which can identify with the characters in his novels, relate fully to their problems, frustrations and struggles, and share their aspirations. The cultural frame of reference is shared by author, publisher and public alike. Herein lies a fundamental difference between Bebey's novels and the pre-independence novels of Oyono, Laye or Beti which are directed primarily towards a European readership. No longer are cultural explanations offered or points of cultural difference avoided in order to facilitate understanding by the non-African. Gone are the tedious tirades against, or heavy satire of, colonialist misdeeds. Now the stress is firmly on the telling of a tale involving ordinary Africans – peasant farmers, fishermen, market vendors, functionaries, businessmen and local sages – faced with personal and social problems largely of their own making.

To remember that these novels are written by an African, about Africans, in Africa, for Africans, helps us to understand why Bebey has ignored such Occidental niceties as aesthetic distance, self-conscious narration, authorial silence and the like. They are alien to his culture. It might of course be argued, as Albert Gerard does in his essay 'Preservation of tradition in African creative writing', that the novel itself is essentially the product of Western civilization, the premises of which are entirely at variance with those of African cultures.[7] Why, then, should the form even be attempted by Africans in search of their authenticity? Bebey feels, in common with many other black artists, that cross-cultural fertilization, besides being an inevitable process, can only enrich his own heritage, and that in marrying the Western novel form to the African oral tradition, something new and dynamic with its own distinctive identity must surely emerge. The novel, in short, will discover its African voice. If Laye, Oyono, Dadié and Beti africanized the *content* of the novel in the 1950s, Bebey's purpose is to complete the work of assimilation by presenting that content in an African *form*, and one, more specifically, drawn from the oral literary tradition of his native Cameroon:

> . . . I rely heavily on the musicians in my country who play the *mvet* and tell stories with it. From time to time, they launch into lengthy poetic descriptions about the forest or whatever. And sometimes, they start speaking as though they were a double personality, two people

speaking to each other . . . There is no transition between the art of
narrating and that of singing or playing music. For me, it's all the same
world. I never knew of any musician back home who didn't tell stories
or recite poems. All of the arts blend together as a unity . . .[8]

This explains why Bebey's narrators try so hard to please, entertain
and be congenial; why they so painstakingly explain events to the reader
in order to ensure that he follows them without effort; and why they are
such gifted performers with their ready quips, witty digressions, lyrical
flights and sense of the dramatic. Such are the stock-in-trade of the
Doualan story-teller with his *mvet*. And like that story-teller, Bebey's
narrators combine comedy, farce, tragedy and overt didacticism freely
together as they portray traditional village and modern urban life. They
reflect the horror, joys, fears and indignation of the reader and serve as
constantly persuasive agents. Of course, they over-indulge him and
undisguisedly manipulate him. Yet this sort of behaviour strikes a
responsive chord in the new, literate African bourgeoisie, be they clerks
and functionaries in Douala and Tamale or students and teachers in Zaria
and Abidjan. Their point of reference is not Henry James, but the local
griot-*conteur* with whose narrative tricks they are thoroughly familiar.
When Mbenda addresses himself directly to the reader and cries 'listen to
me now', the operative word is 'listen'; for his tale is to be listened to like
any other told under the village palaver tree at the end of the day and
orchestrated by enthralled gasps and the occasional crackle of the nearby
fire. These are the perimeters of Mbenda's world, his only frame of
reference. A descendant of Bilé, son of Bessengué, he speaks Douala and
has never read a book. His thousand-year-old tradition is one in which
the telling of a tale, whether about the reign of Bilé over the Akwas or his
own sentimental entanglements, is a social event to be relished by the
collectivity rather than a literary experience to be enjoyed by the individual in isolation. The same may be said of his brother narrator in *Le Roi
Albert d'Effidi* and, though to a diminished degree, of *La Poupée
ashanti*'s market observer. (Such a diminution may be explained by the
fact that the action of this latter novel takes place within an urban
framework and in a foreign country.)

Like all story-tellers worthy of their craft, Bebey's narrators are blessed with a sense of humour and a predilection for irony, and they make
free use of both to protect themselves or their friends, demolish enemies,
uphold village customs, or simply to amuse. Generally, the tone is
light-hearted and quite devoid of that anger and bitterness which perme-
ate the novels of Oyono. Only in *La Poupée ashanti* do we find passages of
high ironic causticity akin to that of *Une Vie de boy*. This is because it

concentrates, much more than the other novels, on diagnosing the ills of the modern African state. The state-controlled radio, corrupt politicians, morally putrefied bureaucrats, inept public scribes, all are targets for the narrator's satirical darts. The latter applauds the work of the government's Commission of Inquiry, the truthfulness of the radio bulletins, and justifies Nkrumah's assumption of dictatorial powers. This technique, dear to Oyono, which consists in defending the manifestly indefensible, constitutes one of Bebey's favourite ironic devices. And in an age of one-party states, presidents-for-life, tight censorship, arbitrary arrest and summary executions, such irony is as necessary a weapon to Bebey as ever it was to Oyono or Voltaire or Montesquieu. He himself has aptly stated the problem: 'With everything that's going on in Africa these days, you have to twist your tongue in all sorts of ways.'[9] It should be noted, however, that unlike these earlier writers, Bebey rarely indulges in authorial irony at the narrator's expense. That is to say, he rarely reduces his narrator to the level of a Candide-like puppet. Instead, narrator and author share the same ironic sense and take a similar pleasure in employing it. At such moments, they merge together as one.

Moreover, since the educational level of Bebey's narrators improves as we progress from *Le Fils d'Agatha Moudio* to *Le Roi Albert d'Effidi*, so the narrator–author distance decreases. Indeed, only in the first of these novels do marked fluctuations exist between the two. This is due, as one might expect, to Mbenda's limited knowledge and narrow background. Furthermore, it is important to remember that the Mbenda-narrator is not the Mbenda-hero of the story. The former, being several years older than the latter, enjoys all the advantages of hindsight and the wisdom that comes with experience. This is why, on occasion, the Mbenda-narrator expresses surprise at or passes judgement on the attitudes of the Mbenda-hero, or even gives advice – on the management of a polygamous household, for instance – which the Mbenda-hero would have done well to follow. To complicate matters, the Mbenda-narrator sometimes relives the experience of his earlier self from that earlier point of view before returning to his more experienced later state to make an editorial comment. The views of this older, wiser Mbenda correspond more closely to those of the author.

Although the Africanization of the novel in Bebey's hands has resulted in the 'griotization' of the narrator, the licence thus acquired cannot be absolute. These modern *conteurs* are still governed by the laws of plausibility. And it is here that we discern certain flaws in Bebey's narrative technique. One of the more obvious stems from his use of a European language to animate the African scene. French is mandatory if his novels are to reach a wide readership and, as such,

remain economically viable. 'I can't use Douala to communicate with
the rest of the world', Bebey protests good-humouredly. 'Sometimes,
I wonder why everyone doesn't learn to speak Doulala!'[10] Moreover,
in common with many other educated Africans, his command of the
French medium is total. But can French *per se* successfully convey
the essence of African thought and civilization? Bebey's answer to
this knotty question is categorical:

> Whether I replace French by Douala is not the point. What matters is
> that I extract the essence of Douala and put it alongside the essence of
> French so as to attain a very enriched cultural level. It's not a technical
> problem but a cultural one . . .[11]

If we accept Bebey's argument, what we are required to judge is not
the author's choice of language, European or African, but rather *how* he
uses it. In other words, does he use the French language with sufficient
skill accurately to convey the African essence of his characters? The
answer in Bebey's case must be 'no'. His Douala- *(Agatha Moudio, Albert
d'Effidi)*, Ashanti- and Fon-speaking *(La Poupée ashanti)* characters are,
by and large, uneducated folk. Like most people of their social level, they
would undoubtedly be given to ungrammatical speech patterns, vulgar-
ity, a restricted vocabulary, and employ colourful images and axioms
drawn from the rich storehouse of their respective vernaculars. (Com-
pare the English of Petticoat Lane or the French of Marseilles's dockland
or the Arabic of the Tunis souks.) In attempting to re-create the African
essence, the writer must not only communicate his characters' attitudes,
value and priorities (which Bebey does very well), but also the subtleties
of their indigenous speech: their peculiar rhythms, images, repetitions,
and so forth. Bebey largely refuses this challenge. He allows his characters and narrators, regardless of social rank or educational background,
to converse in the most impeccably grammatical French. With never a
word of slang, never a muddled articulation, their speeches have a ring of
artificiality which leaves the reader with a curious sense of loss.

A narrator's excessive flexibility also undermines his plausibility.
Such is the case in Bebey's first two novels. Mbenda and the third-person
narrator of *La Poupée ashanti* seem unable or unwilling to maintain their
stance, to narrate their stories within the limits Bebey has set for them.
Mbenda's recording eye darts about everywhere, now inside one character, now inside another. Their intimate thoughts and opinions are an
open book to him. 'Mbaka had come to meet with the hunters knowing
perfectly well that if his efforts came to nothing he would have to stay
closetted at home for a few days', we are informed in the first chapter.
Similarly, the Accra Market narrator tells us why Mam sighs or swallows

hard, why Edna lowers her eyes, or how she really feels about her grandmother's awkward questions. Sometimes, these narrators hover with omniscient detachment over the proceedings before scurrying back into their subjective states to comment, summarize or advise. At other moments, they become so engrossed in recording a character's opinions, they are literally assimilated into his being and we see reality momentarily from that other narrowly subjective point of view. Nor does Mbenda's first-person stance seem to preclude his knowing about those situations he could never have witnessed, such as the initial encounter between Mbaka and Moudiki in the former's hut, the bride-price negotiations at Tanga's house or the ultra-confidential ritual performed by Mother Evil-Eye on Fanny in the darkness of the old sorceress's hut.

These repeated shifts, this power to expand or contract perception, this right to intermittent knowledge are hallmarks of the griot-*conteur*'s technique, and they are responsible for the polytonality of Bebey's work. His artistry is at its shakiest, however, when he discards his narrative agent altogether in order either to let the characters and action take care of themselves or directly to assume that agent's functions himself. In the first situation, that of the narrative void, the characters take command and speak to each other uninterruptedly as in a dramatic performance. In Chapters 2, 8, 11 and 13 of *La Poupée ashanti*, dialogue dominates and outside commentary or supporting description is reduced almost to nil. The device is most effective in revealing the psychological states and social attitudes of the main characters with maximum pace and intensity. Chapter 2, consisting of two dialogues, provides an excellent illustration. But the dangers are enormous, particularly when the characters are superficial and the issues involved trivial. How to raise the platitudinous to the level of high art is Bebey's constant dilemma. The argument between Mam and Aunt Princess in Chapter 13 over the question of Edna's marriage could, for instance, have been reported adequately by the narrator in one neat paragraph. As it stands, it merely confirms the truism that nature is good to imitate, but not to the point of boredom. Bebey's characters, like those of Dickens, exist largely through the words they themselves utter. But the crucial question of what to summarize and what to heighten is never satisfactorily resolved in his novels.

Bebey's usurpation of his narrator's functions stems from the difference in their educational levels. Since that difference is most pronounced in *Le Fils d'Agatha Moudio*, it is in that novel that the usurpation most frequently occurs. Near the end of the book, Mbenda eloquently compares the beauty of the innocent child with the ugliness of the adult sullied by his prejudices, and makes a plea for understanding which

alone can secure peace and happiness in the world. This Wouri fisherman possesses neither the resources of vocabulary nor the profundity of
intellect to generate such phrases as 'the nullity of the races', 'epidermal
defects' or even 'classes of pariahs', no matter how maturative his
experience may have been. Pitched at a much higher intellectual level
than the rest of the narrative, this passage marks the author's personal
entry onstage to pronounce the moral of the story before bringing down
the curtain. Similar authorial intrusions may be detected in *La Poupée
ashanti* where the narrator makes a brief reference to Schubert's 'The
Trout' and to certain practices inside French movie-theatres.

Bebey's dilemma is that he needs a grass-roots narrator in order to
re-create the rural peasant and urban market scenes with maximum
intensity, that is, from their very centre. At the same time, he needs a
narrator with sufficient education and cultural understanding to allow
scope for the articulation of Bebey's philosophy in Bebey's own terms.
Unfortunately, such incompatible states of being cannot be found
inside the same skin. This is why Bebey feels obliged at certain moments
to push his narrators aside, abolish all aesthetic distance, and speak
directly to his readers as an African intellectual concerning matters dear
to his heart. In short, he temporarily abandons his craft as a novelist to
mount the soap-box of the moralist-teacher. His artistic stature is
thereby impaired.

Happily, the narrative inconsistencies in the earlier novels are largely
corrected in *Le Roi Albert d'Effidi* where Bebey achieves a greater degree
of tonal unity. Since the narrator is an educated observer like the author
himself, the gap between them can contract to total identification without causing any great disruption of tone. The central characters – King
Albert, Toutouma, Bikounou – are likewise endowed with sufficient
intelligence, perception, experience or knowledge of the modern world
to reflect Bebey's own views while retaining their credibility. Moreover,
the fact that the novel is set in the period immediately prior to Cameroonian independence and firmly focused on traditional village life also
allows Bebey to avoid what might otherwise have been an irresistible
temptation to hurl invectives against Ahidjo's regime. Despite the
increased sophistication of both narrator and principal characters, *Le Roi
Albert d'Effidi* has lost nothing of the freshness and spontaneity we
associate with the Douala musician-story-teller. This is why it must
be considered Bebey's most artistically successful novel to date.

The road towards a perfected African novelistic expression remains
long. But Bebey has pointed the way. It lies – as does African authenticity
itself – in the fusion of Occidental and indigenous forms. And that fusion

will be purely on Africa's terms. As Bebey puts it in *Le Roi Albert d'Effidi*:

... The essential question is to know whether, yes or no, Africans are to be left free to practise the kind of literature, music, painting, dancing, or mass of their choice, rather than the kind that appeals to this or that scholar in search of pernicious examples of exotic art. And above all, why stop Africans today from following the methods of artistic creation which others formerly forced them to learn on the pretext that those methods were better than their own?

References
1. Bebey's statement to this writer during an interview in Paris on 20 August 1977. For the original French version of this interview, see *Présence francophone*, 16 (Université de Sherbrooke, Québec, Canada).
2. *Le Fils d'Agatha Moudio* (Yaoundé, Editions CLE, 1967); translated as *Agatha Moudio's Son* by Joyce A. Hutchinson (London, Heinemann, 1971). All references to Bebey's works in this essay are from the Yaounde edition and in the author's translation.
3. *La Poupée ashanti* (Yaounde, Editions CLE, 1973); translated as *The Ashanti Doll* by Joyce A. Hutchinson (New York, Lawrence Hill, 1977 and Heinemann, London 1978).
4. Le Roi Albert d'Effidi (Yaoundé, Editions CLE, 1976). An English version of this novel is presently under consideration by Lawrence Hill.
5. In private conversation, Bebey has confided that he conceives of him as a journalist.
6. Initially, however, this choice was fortuitous. 'I happened to be in Yaoundé, noticed they had a publishing house and saw no reason why I shouldn't try them', recounts Bebey. 'So I gave them *Le Fils d'Agatha Moudio*. Two years later, it was published . . . After that, I thought I should stay with CLE. Although I wasn't living in Cameroon, it allowed me to participate in the country's cultural life'. (Interview of 20 August 1977.)
7. *Research in African Literature*, I, 1 (1970), p. 37.
8. Paris interview, 20 August, 1977.
9. ibid. This also explains why Bebey has practically ceased all journalistic activities – a field in which he refuses to indulge in tongue-twisting: 'As a journalist, I'm not prepared to write only those things that will please. I have to say what needs to be said' (same interview).
10. Paris interview, 20 August 1977. Bebey has written a number of poems in the Douala language. They remain as yet unpublished.
11. ibid.

Index

▼▼▼▼▼▼▼▼▼▼▼▼▼▼▼▼▼▼▼▼▼▼▼▼▼▼▼▼▼▼▼▼▼▼▼▼▼▼